The Limits of Foreign Policy

The $\boxed{\text{Limits}}$ of

Foreign Policy

by Charles Burton Marshall

Henry Holt and Company · New York

Foreword

The students of this college generation have been subjected to widespread and violent discussions of the foreign policies and external relations of these United States. The claims and counterclaims, charges and countercharges, have left students and the general public with an extremely shaky foundation for judgment about some of the most serious questions of our day.

The obvious danger in this situation led us to search for a lecturer who could be trusted to give our college community a sane and firm platform of fact and theory for understanding foreign policy. Our inquiries finally directed us to Charles Burton Marshall, who at the time of these lectures was a member of the Policy Planning Staff of the State Department.

As Mr. Marshall delivered his lectures, it became clear to all of us that we were privileged to hear the results of a fine and competent mind dealing with intricate problems

5

that affect the lives of every man, woman, and child in this country. Because we found Mr. Marshall's thought so stimulating and important, we requested that the substance of the lectures be published.

These lectures were given at Hollins College in honor of Bessie Carter Randolph, a long-time student of international relations, a distinguished professor of this subject, and the president of Hollins College from 1933 to 1950. She joins the faculty and trustees of the college in their desire that this significant contribution receive the wide and thoughtful audience it so clearly merits.

John R. Everett
PRESIDENT, HOLLINS COLLEGE

Author's Note

The invitation to give five lectures at Hollins College stipulated United States foreign policy as the subject. My initial intention was to treat narratively some of the crucial decisions in foreign policy of recent years. This would require explaining the goals in forming the decisions. In the process of turning this over in my mind during the spring of 1953, the further need of some attention to the limits bearing on the establishment of such goals became clear. By September of 1953, the time for composition, this preliminary aspect relating to the limits had grown to encompass all the rest. The lectures were given in the fall of 1953. In the following January I made some rhetorical revisions preparatory to publication. The temptation to take advantage of the interval by writing in some hindsights to give evidence of forethought was strong, but I overcame it.

Charles Burton Marshall

Contents

The Limits of Foreign Policy

I

Nobody, in fact, who has had occasion actually to witness history in the making, and to observe how infrequent and adventitious is the part played in great affairs by "policy" or planned intention, can believe thereafter that history is ever quite so simple, or quite so deliberate, as it seems in retrospect; or that the apparent relation between cause and effect was the relation which at the time, and in the circumstances, actually determined the course of affairs. . . . Nobody who has not watched "policy" expressing itself in day to day action can realize how seldom is the course of events determined by deliberately planned purpose. . . .

—HAROLD NICOLSON, *The Congress of Vienna*

The Limits of
Foreign Policy

One of the most unforgettable characters I have never met
is archy—spelled with a lower-case *a*—the philosophic roach,
creature of the imagination of Don Marquis. I recall as an
example of this roach's insight an account of a conversation
with another insect about the difficulties of livelihood
among cockroaches in the face of such circumstances as
stringency of food and the unremitting hostility of man,
whose hand and sometimes also his foot are against them.
The other insect suggests a formula for freedom from want
and freedom from fear for cockroaches. This calls for them
to quit the towns for the countryside and there to become
grasshoppers. At first the simplicity of this suggested solution astounds the roach. Then second thought prompts a
request for precise directions for the transformation into
grasshoppers. The other insect answers, in sum, that this is
a detail for the execution of policy; the general scheme has
been indicated, and it is up to others to give it effect, for

policy-makers should not have to do everything. The roach sets all this down under the title of "statesmanship," with a suggestion that the account has in it "something analogous to a number of easy schemes for the improvement of the human race."

It does indeed bear such analogy. Nothing comes more easily or does less good than the engaging pastime of thinking up bold and imaginative schemes for improvement in disregard of the means for realizing them. This is true in all human endeavor. Here I wish to apply the thought to the subject of foreign policy.

I do not need to exhort about the importance of this subject. Foreign policy has a bearing on the duration and the conditions of our lives as individuals. It bears also on profound questions of our destiny as a nation, for the relationships between us and the portions of the world external to our jurisdiction will largely determine whether our national greatness is to be enduring or brief.

That issue is not foreclosed in our favor. No grace inherent in us and no providential gift exempt us from the pitfalls and infirmities attending the course of great nations. Whether, and how long, we shall avoid them will depend in some great and essential portion on our courage and wisdom as a politically organized people in handling our relationships with other peoples in other lands with cultures and loyalties different from ours.

Surely here is a subject of such moment as to deserve our taking great care in thinking about it and discussing it.

Foreign policy does not always receive such care. Indeed it is altogether too often denied it. The sweep of its problems gives foreign policy a special attraction for those—in the words of Shelley's self-description—born with a passion to reform the world. Foreign policy appeals to those inspired by identification with large and high-sounding public causes. Its complexities and subtleties are rich with opportunity for generalizers and obfuscators.

This is consequential. Ours is an accountable government. Acceptability to popular opinion is certainly a factor in the conduct of foreign policy by our government. Popular opinion is not of much, if any, value in helping in the discovery of answers to the problems in this field. It certainly counts, however, in setting bounds to the area of maneuver available to those charged with responsibility. A sound general understanding of the limits of foreign policy, avoiding excessive expectations and the sense of frustration incident to the disappointment of such expectations, is therefore essential to the conduct of a sound foreign policy.

I do not mean to identify lack of public comprehension as the sole brake on progress along wise courses in foreign policy. If it were that, then all that would be necessary in order to achieve wisdom and success would be to do away with accountability in our government and to let magistrates and experts take over unconditional authority with respect to external relations. Magistrates are never worthy of such mastery, however, and experts are never endowed with such expertness. Those who govern and those who counsel them are subject to refractions of view and errors of judgment. The problem is neither how to endow them with unquestioned authority in foreign affairs nor how to render them entirely subservient to the whims and pressures of the particular interests which in sum constitute the public. The problem is how to acquaint Americans in general, whether in government or out of it, with the inherent limits respecting foreign policy so that issues may turn on questions how best for the nation to fill the limits rather than on vain propositions of perfection and destructive self-reproach over failure to achieve it.

I intend in these discourses to put calipers on foreign policy. I wish to stress its limits rather than its magnitudes. In this first I shall do so analytically, concentrating on the inherent character of the subject. In the second I shall trace briefly our past. I shall stress the effects of its peculiar characteristics in forming the bright and wide expectations of Americans in regard to their country's role in the world. The third discourse will recount how circumstances external to the nation have changed enormously in our times and have imposed on us the necessity of revising the attitudes toward world affairs made habitual in our historic past. The fourth will examine the importance of the concept of limitation in foreign policy in relation to the issues dividing the world in the present. The final one will be an exercise in hindsight on some of the undertakings in foreign policy resulting from inflated hopes in combination with depressed critical faculties during the half-century or so since our nation attained the status of a great power.

As a beginning in laboring the analytic aspects, a loose definition will do. The foreign policy of a state takes form in the courses of action undertaken by authority of the state and intended to affect situations beyond the span of its jurisdiction.

Do not construe too narrowly the meaning of the word *action*. In this field utterance is sometimes a form of action, and pronouncements are deeds when they convey meaning about things intended to be done rather than merely expressing abstractions and moralizations.

Let me emphasize the human and therefore finite character of the political institutions concerned in foreign policy.

The state is an abstract expression representing a body of people occupying a defined territory and politically organized so as to be capable of acting collectively with respect to matters both within that territory and beyond it. Government is the apparatus of decision and execution for such action.

The terms *state* and *government* convey ideas of hugeness, majesty, and impersonality. These overtones should not mislead us. The state—and this is true also of its agent, government—remains, in Plato's phrase, man written large. It is only man. It is not superman. It is man written large, not limitless. The individual is multiplied in the frame of the state. The individual's limitations are not transcended. The institutions of political life do not add to the dimensions of the human mind. They have no insights denied to individuals. They produce no wisdom beyond the compass of man's mind. The intelligence operating in the lines of decision and execution is but human intelligence. It has the inherent attributes of contingency, fallibility, and subjectivity. Service to the state does not bring to the minds of the servants any additional endowments for perceiving the future. For all its majesty, the situation of the state is still the human situation.

Americans generally recognize the characteristics of intrinsic limitation in respect to the state's role in domestic affairs. Here indeed, in their precepts if not so much in their practices, the Americans are virtually singular among the nations for their skepticism about the wisdom and the efficacy of public authority. Americans tend to overlook these limitations—at least, many Americans tend to do so—in their attitudes toward the role of the United States in foreign affairs. In this range their perspectives tend to be thrown off. Americans, said Gertrude Stein, are brought up "to believe in boundlessness." With respect to nothing else is this so manifest as it is with respect to their views as to the inherent capability of the United States government to avail in matters actually external to its jurisdiction and therefore beyond its control.

I stress the obvious but often overlooked externalness of foreign policy. The fundamental circumstance giving rise to foreign policy is that most of the world is outside the United States. The areas in which our foreign policy has its effects are those lying beyond the range of our law. They include about fifteen-sixteenths of the world's land surface and contain about sixteen-seventeenths of its peoples. We cannot ordain the conditions there. The forces do not respond to our fiat. At best we can only affect them. We exercise only influence, not the sovereign power to dispose, in those ranges once described by the Supreme Court in a memorable opinion as "this vast external realm, with its important, complicated, delicate, and manifold problems."

I can recall from my own experience dozens of examples of the American tendency to disregard limitation of power precisely with respect to matters beyond the limits of our control.

An exigent lady in the audience in a Midwestern city about three years ago asked me to outline the course of United States foreign policy for the next ten years. I denied having a crystal ball. She reduced to five years the interval concerned in the request. I carefully restated my view of foreign policy as necessarily being in large part a response to situations arising beyond the national jurisdiction and therefore beyond our government's control and beyond my modest power to predict. She spurned that answer. She insisted on the predictability of the future in world affairs, given sufficient diligence on the part of those conducting policy. I told her the main surely predictable element of the future was trouble, which was bound to proliferate along our course, though I could not undertake to define all its forms and occasions. The lady answered with scorn for the Department of State for not having worked out a formula for eliminating trouble.

Such ideas abound within as well as outside the government. I recall, for example, a conference of a couple of years ago between a delegation from another office of the government and the members of the Policy Planning Staff of the State Department. The visitors wanted to mesh with foreign policy certain plans of their making. They asked us to unroll the secret scrolls of the future—at least for a twenty-year interval of it. They departed in dudgeon, disdain, and disbelief on hearing our disclaimer.

I call to mind being asked by a man in an audience in Texas a few months ago to explain the State Department's failure to foresee the rising clash in interest and purpose between metropolitan France and native elements of French North Africa. I assured him this had been foreseen. Then he asked for an accounting on the United States' failure to prevent it.

In the life of the state as in the life of the individual, problems foreseen may often be beyond the scope of one's power of ordaining. The situation in the conduct of foreign policy often reminds me of the story of the boastful pilot. While steering a ship into port, he remarked to the skipper, "I know every rock in this harbor." A rending contact between ship and reef interrupted him. Then he added, "That's one of them now." I related all this to my questioner in Texas but did not convince him that the fact of a falling out between North African Arabs and France was not due to some remissness in Washington.

A while back a friend of mine, giving me his personal views on how to handle foreign affairs, drew an analogy from his own business, railroad traffic management. He represented the world as a switchyard, the United States as a locomotive, and all the other nations as boxcars. I remarked on the irrelevancy of his account of railroading technics to foreign affairs. The world is not an organized place like a switchyard. Other nations are not inert vehicles like boxcars. They are corporate entities with purposes of their own. Respecting them the United States disposes no monopoly of power like that of a locomotive among boxcars. All this I explained to my friend. He rejoined with a comment about the mulish unwillingness of the members of the State Department to accept from other walks of life the lessons of how to conduct the nation's affairs.

The same notion of the attainability of perfect foresight in the planning and perfect efficacy in the execution of foreign policy is an ingredient in the abundant schemes put forth by well-meaning groups for a variety of one-shot solutions of the problems of a difficult world. It is reflected also in a way many people have of attributing developments in every quadrant of the globe to some design conceived in Washington.

This underlies a great deal of discussion about the China issue. One hears repeated references to our having lost China—a land never ours to lose. That ancient, complex, and populous land is represented as without a substance of its own—as merely a screen reflecting only what is projected from this side of the Pacific. The course of that remote nation is construed as wholly determinable by American will. From the tone of discussion one might never guess that indigenous impulses and predispositions counted for anything in China's course: for the native army's want of military zeal someone here must be held to account; for an Oriental regime's loss of grip on itself blame must be fixed in Washington.

This mistaken notion of thinking of our policy as the paramount factor in situations beyond our borders is not confined to the China issue. I have heard serious-minded Americans lay at our own doorstep the blame for everything believed by them to be deficient in the internal situations of the Latin American nations. Three learned gentlemen with whom I dined recently spent much of the evening discussing how the United States must go about curing what they called the emotional sicknesses in the political societies of Western Europe—all with the assumption that the states of mind of other peoples were amenable to our sovereign disposition.

I believe it worth while to ponder briefly the causes of this tendency to see in disproportion the dimensions of our power in the world, a tendency highly important as a main obstacle to sound thinking about foreign policy.

According to a friend of mine professionally concerned with the study of deeper sources of human behavior, this tendency of individuals to think of the state as if it were omnipotent in the world is an unconsciously chosen way of redressing the sense of their own inadequacy, much as small boys redress their boyishness by vaunting the imagined prowess of their fathers. I shall leave such theory to others better prepared than I to delve into the psyche.

One source of the notion of perfect efficacy in foreign affairs, it seems to me, is consciousness of an extraordinarily successful past—something to be discussed in my next discourse. The diplomatic course in the evolution from a colonial beachhead to a power of highest magnitude was one of matchless performance. It is easy to assume this as setting the enduring standard for our conduct in the world.

Faith in law—perhaps I should say excessive faith in legislation—is another factor relevant here. Legislation is law. Law is to be obeyed. An aim legislatively expressed is *ipso facto* achievable. So goes the reasoning. This tempts toward exaggerated notions of the preventive as well as of the positive power of legislation. In both respects this has a bearing on ideas about foreign policy. In the Congress the same voices may be raised both on behalf of peremptory propositions to impel Europeans toward the constitutional venture of integration—as if peremptoriness availed in such matters—and for undertakings to exempt our own practices from the altering influence of foreign affairs by veering back toward the modes of the Articles of Confederation. The question of consistency between two such proposals reminds me of the time I heard a quartet in a contrapuntal arrangement of "Sailing Over the Bounding Main" and "River, Stay Away from My Door."

Uncritical faith in the efficacy of legislation in its positive aspects has a particular relevance in the phase of extensive grants-in-aid to other countries. I used to note this in the time of my service as consultant to the Committee on Foreign Affairs of the House of Representatives. In executive sessions of the committee and in conferences on legislation with their senatorial counterparts, the more zealous members would contend over the tones of adjectives, the nuances of nouns, and the degrees of activity implicit in the verbs going into congressional statements of policy accompanying legislation in the field of foreign affairs. In such arguments the atmosphere often seemed charged with the import of destiny. It was as if the issues of history were being settled by verbalization.

The very fact of having a lot of legislation laying down the objectives entertained by the Congress for situations internal to other countries tends to obscure the limits of our jurisdiction—to make us forget that we cannot by our own fiat cure problems arising from the narrowness of the margins of political power within other countries or ordain the easy and immediate consummation of purposes realizable, if at all, only with energetic and purposeful support of other peoples in long spans of time.

Another influence on the American attitude toward foreign affairs might be called faith in engineering—confidence of a limitless power to transform situations by working on the material factors, faith in the achievability of great purposes through applying technics. This relates to our natural pride in the physical development of our country. Popular tradition treasures the notion in the realm of creation all things are possible to those who will them. A recent book by an American assailing his government for suffering the postwar contretemps in Germany dismisses the notion of limitation of American power with the observation, "Americans can do anything." The margins available to us have made this true at least in a poetic sense in the development of our own country. The error arises in the attempt to apply it to situations involving wills other than our own.

This faith in capability to transform through material factors is relevant to a tendency to think loosely about the nature of force, which is physical, and its relation to power in general. By force I mean the capacity to transmit energy and so to expend it as to do vital harm to a foe and also the deterrent, compulsive effect produced by having that capacity. It is only one of many forms of power. For power let us use Count Tolstoi's definition of it as "merely the relation between the expression of someone's will and the execution of that will by others."

Wars occur when nations seek to impose their wills by effecting drastic changes in the ratios of power through radical action in the factors of force. The force factors are susceptible of precision in military planning. The elements are concrete. The speeds of ships, their capabilities for carrying men and cargo, the distances, the fuel requirements of planes and tanks, the fire power of divisions, and so on are knowable factors. The military planning process, insofar as it relates to the ponderables of real or hypothetical campaigns, turns out tidy and complete results. I do not mean that battles and campaigns are fought according to preconceived schedules. I mean only that insofar as advance planning is employed in the military field, the quotients are precise, the columns are even, and the conclusions concrete.

In a course of active hostilities force capabilities may be brought to a ratio of 100 to 0 as between one side and the other by the elimination of resistance in a particular place for a particular time, changing the relationship between antagonists to that between victor and vanquished. Surrender may be complete and unconditional. Victory may appear absolute.

It is easy for the unwary to jump to a conclusion that if all human affairs were laid out with the precision of military plans, then all problems could be brought to as complete solution as can the problem of force in the conduct of a victorious military campaign.

Victory's appearance of absoluteness is transitory. Victory itself is evanescent. It invariably has given way to a substitute unless the victors, like the Romans at Carthage, have obliterated the conquered or undertaken permanently to deprive them of will—in other words, to enslave them, an undertaking likely to prove burdensome and fearsome to the enslavers as well as to the enslaved.

Ascendancy based on force begins to diminish as soon as force ceases to be sole arbiter. The introduction of factors other than force modifies the relationship between conquerors and those conquered. The victor will ceases to be the only active will. The vanquished recover in some degree wills of their own. A mutuality of relationship begins to be renewed. The relationship recovers political character. Victory fades as a circumstance and becomes only a memory. Bold expectations identified with the moment of victory fade away with it.

This accounts for an ancient and recurring cliché—I am old enough to have heard it in the sequels to two world wars—about politicians' having dissipated the glories and benefits of victories achieved by violence. To my view a failure of events to confirm expectations shows something wrong about the expectations rather than something deficient in the facts. The failure of peace to live up to the high hopes of the moment of victory shows something to be deceptive about the hopes—indeed about the concept—of victory itself.

Use of force is an incident. The problems of power are endless. Wars occur. Politics endures. Let us identify as a persistent illusion about power in foreign policy the idea that by dint of planning and perseverance it can be realized in that degree of efficacy seemingly secured in the moment of victory. It is an illusion first in equating all power with force and second in exaggerating the enduring effectiveness of the latter.

In examining the urges and the claims of perfection of solution in foreign policy, let us take note of a characteristic tendency of our times to regard the whole field of human relations as substantively and entirely an aspect of science. This links with a notion of the capability of cumulative and organized knowledge to solve anything and an accompanying view of every problem as something by definition solvable. If not creative scientific thinkers themselves, then certainly popularizers of scientific achievement have nurtured this idea. Whatever the applicability in material relations, the concept is misleading when applied as a universal.

I call to mind a statement of august auspices: "In social science in its broadest sense, which is concerned with the relations of men in society and with the conditions of social order and well being, we have learned only an adumbration of the laws which govern these vastly complex phenomena." That is part of a pronouncement by the American Association of University Professors in 1915 in advocacy of academic freedom. The case for nonrestriction in the study of human affairs here is simply that mankind has not yet done all the homework to be done. The concept of truth implicit here is of something not yet fully mastered rather than something ever unfolding and therefore beyond formulation.

That statement echoed in my consciousness a few days ago in a conversation with a young man regarded as a comer in the field—perhaps I should say the nebula—of psychological warfare. He assured me of such developments ahead in the science of psychology as would afford complete prediction of human responses to verbal stimuli and enable the exercise of complete mastery over mankind's future, presenting the prospect of making and keeping all men free by pouring the right words into their ears. According to him, all this would be realized with the closing of the interval by which social sciences lag behind the natural sciences, placing the problems of man's behavior on a footing with the problems of environment and rendering them completely subject to control by technics. "The manipulation of men's minds" is the horrible phrase he used.

The prospect set forth involves ingenious paradox. Who would manipulate the minds of the manipulators while the manipulators were busy manipulating minds? Choice being the condition of freedom, how could men be said to be free if deprived by mental manipulation of the possibility of being anything else than free? These questions were not germane or important to the young psychological warrior. He looked forward to the sovereignty of propagandists with a professional self-assurance equal to that of the philosopher Plato's proposal of the kingship of philosophers like himself as a formula for political perfection.

The notion of the power of scientific reason to solve all the problems of our age relates to a habit of mind derived from the study of history. To this I wish to give special emphasis.

The whole continuum of time and space, in all its vastness and variety, far exceeds the compass of any finite mind. Only an infinite consciousness could understand all of it and perceive the lines of relationship among all the entities and all the occurrences within its scope. With his limitations, the individual can work his intelligence only on small portions of it. Within segments comprehensible to him and from his particular standpoint, he observes or construes relationships between one phenomenon and another. In the measure of his understanding he tries to analyze these as lines of cause and effect. From these he seeks to derive principles for comprehending and controlling his environment. This in general is the method of science.

I am concerned here only with its application to history. The historian turns his powers of inquiry and analysis onto some segment of space and some range of past time manageable within his intellectual compass. From what is available to him of the residual record, he infers lines of causation. He distills his knowledge and sorts it into chapters and volumes presenting the essences, as he understands them, of the eras and areas subjected to his analysis.

This is legitimate and necessary intellectual endeavor. To its results, however, one must always take care to apply proper reservations. The past did not actually unfold in chapters and volumes. Its emerging realities were never as compact and crystallized as they are made to appear by the craftsmanship of the historian. The participants in past events never enjoyed those clear vistas marked for us by the historian along the lines of cause and effect. To the contemporaries the proportions in any epoch were very different from what they appear to us in long retrospection.

Besides this tendency to confuse the history with the reality of the past—besides the notion that the residue we retain is the whole and the essence of any departed epoch—let us take note of the notion that history unfolds according to some logical scheme, the whole of which is inferable from any of its parts, much as an archaeologist contrives to reconstruct an entire skeleton from a few stray bones. This is the notion that from history we can derive the key to the future. This is the notion that by sufficient diligence we can lay down the lines of what is to come as neatly and definitively as the systematic historian seems to plot out the lines of what has gone before.

It is only a step from this concept to the idea of manipulating the future. If the pattern of the future is ascertainable by human intelligence, then its determinative elements must be discoverable by human intelligence also, and by pre-empting control of these and working them according to its own will, a human agency can take charge of destiny. So the idea goes.

This notion of finding and working the push-buttons and levers controlling the future involves a great contradiction between two concepts—on the one hand, the deterministic idea of an ascertainable pattern of the future and on the other the concept of the possibility of perfect freedom of will involved in the assumption that a mortal entity can gain ascendancy over the future and make it responsive to its desires as a machine responds to a guiding hand. This notion makes man and his mind, his will, and his institutions on the one hand the puppets of a foreclosed destiny. On the other hand it presumes to place the controlling cords in the hands of human agency.

George Santayana's words caution us against reliance on any special school of thought "which squints and overlooks half the facts and half the difficulties in its eagerness to find in some detail the key to the whole." This fallacy resides in every undertaking to formulate a system about the past and then to apply it to gain mastery over the future. It inheres in every notion of an exclusive formula for being right in human affairs and in every overweening claim to the possession of that formula. It is implicit in every exhortation for us to meet the Communist threat by adopting a system matching that of the adversary in its pretensions to universality and to possession of the keys to the future.

Anyone who has dealt responsibly with foreign policy must have felt the meaning of Whitman's lines:

> How can I pierce the impenetrable blank of the
>   future?
> I feel thy ominous greatness, evil as well as good;
> I watch thee, advancing, absorbing the present,
>   transcending the past;
> I see thy light lighting and thy shadows shadow-
>   ing, as if the entire globe;
> But I do not undertake to define thee—hardly to
>   comprehend thee . . .

To perceive the great extent to which a foreign policy, attempting to cope with the future, must be speculative and chancy is not a source of weakness. To the contrary, in Edmund Burke's phrase, "We can never walk surely but by being sensible of our blindness." The gravest errors are consequent from deceiving oneself that it is possible by some prodigy of planning to overcome this inherent circumstance.

Something of this fallacy is basic to every proposition for a perfect, all-embracing solution of our problems in foreign relations. The young Gladstone's mentor advised him that politics was an unsatisfactory business and that he would have to learn to put up with imperfect results. That advice has wisdom akin to the lessons of *Faust* and *Paradise Lost*: that grace derives from a sense of one's limitations and that tragedy is the wage of losing that sense.

Not perfection but utility is the test of planning in a foreign policy, and utility is a modest virtue. Perhaps an illustration from another field, military operations, properly applies here. The Duke of Wellington once referred to the differences in concept and planning between his adversary and himself in the Peninsular Campaign. The French plans, he said, were made with logical perfection and completeness. He likened them to a fine leather harness—admirable and useful until some part broke, whereupon the whole was useless. His own plans, he said, were made on the principle of rope, and as portions broke under the stress of circumstance, he would just tie knots and go on. A foreign policy should be planned on that principle.

Foresight in foreign policy—the planning function, I might call it—is best if seasoned with contingency and a recognition of human limitation. To set proper perspectives, let us take account not only of the finiteness of the state and of the point that the areas concerned in foreign policy lie beyond the span of national jurisdiction, but also of another point implicit in the definition of foreign policy which I gave at the outset. I refer to the essential relationship between foreign policy and action.

At the risk of sounding very academic, I shall labor this with some more definitions. I do not claim exclusive correctness for them. I set them forth only to insure understanding of my use of the terms.

The situation of the state—substitute the term *government* or *nation* if you will—is that of having some, but only some, capability. That is the situation of responsibility. It lies between the extremes of omnipotence and powerlessness. Each of these extremes alike carries no responsibility.

The situation of responsibility involves the necessity of choice. Choice is simply the selection of one possibility to the exclusion of others when no more than one is feasible. Choice inevitably involves renunciation. In the view of the scholastic philosophers, even an infinite being is compelled to make choices because of being unable to will into existence simultaneously inherently contradictory things. Finite entities have to make choices not only as between inherently contradictory possibilities but also as between things which together are practicably unfeasible within the means at hand.

One knows this from the daily circumstances of his own life—the continuing necessity of allocating one's time and rationing one's money, one's inability to spend the same two hours in both studying and going to the movies, and the incapacity to obtain together the rewards of diligence and the comforts of indolence. One must repeatedly put aside one desirable thing in preference for another thing also desirable. This circumstance distinguishes the real life from the myths treasured in childhood with their seven-league boots, lamps of Aladdin, magic carpets, and open sesames.

The situation of the state in its external responsibilities is that of the limits of adult reality, notwithstanding that many Americans persist in talking of foreign policy in a frame of reference akin to the wishful tales of childhood. Let us apply then to the state in its external relations the simple concepts about will applicable to other human endeavors.

Will is the faculty for making choices. The difference between a weak and a determined will is simply a difference in steadfastness in carrying through with the renunciations inescapably involved in making choices. This is as true in the frame of the state as it is in other human affairs.

An exercise of will is a volition. A volition unfolds at three levels. The first of these concerns motives. By that term I mean those impulses rising from some inner need or desire and spurring the mind to volition. The second level involves ends. By an end I mean that which the mind conceives as representing the satisfaction of the need or desire identified as the source of motivation. The third level involves intentions. At this level the mind adds to the conception of ends the projection of action in pursuit of them.

Note that I say pursuit, not attainment. The capacity of the mind to conceive ends is limitless. The means at hand are invariably limited. The level of intention involves above all the establishment of a balance between ends and means—that is, if one is responsible in his undertakings. Balancing ends and means requires at any juncture the selection of some feasible fraction of one's ends to be acted upon and the deferment of the rest. The portions of one's ends selected for action let us call purposes.

All this applies to foreign policy.

The formulation of foreign policy, if done responsibly, must be regarded as the forming of our intentions—as distinguished from our ends—regarding the world external to our national jurisdiction. The distinction makes a difference. The sum of the foreign policy is the sum not of things we should like to achieve but of the things we do or are going to set about doing in the world. Foreign policy is not the business, in words of Kipling, of

> Thinking of beautiful things we know,
> Dreaming of deeds that we mean to do,
> All complete, in a minute or two—

Something noble, and grand and good,
Done by merely wishing we could.

Many—one finds them in government as well as out of it—
regard foreign policy as a set of good wishes and high aspi-
rations about the world, as that and nothing more. That
sort of thinking relates to foreign policy as cheer-leading
to quarterbacking or as the sum of a man's New Year's
resolutions to his biography.

I do not mean to decry the essentiality of a set of goals
in foreign policy. Ultimate purposes have a value in serving as a standard for knowing how to proceed, problem by
problem, in this field. Moreover, the good is not always
beyond reach, though the way to it is arduous, long, and
charged with paradoxes.

A few years ago one of our most distinguished military
leaders, one typifying in the best sense the combination of
soldiery and statesmanship, made a speech about the cri-
teria for our relationships with the rest of the world. His
peroration was a plea for the nation to guide by the eter-
nal stars instead of steering by the lights of each passing
ship. The sweep and grandeur of his metaphor impressed
me. I said so in a conversation with a seafaring friend. "Obviously you don't know much about the sea," he told me.
"One of the easiest parts of seamanship is celestial naviga-
tion. That never keeps you awake on the bridge all night.
The test of seamanship is the shoals, the fogs, the storms
that blow and yet you can't do anything to stop them, and
the passing ships. Just try to imagine sailing under a skipper who thinks the big part of his job is star-gazing."

That anecdote makes my point. The goal aspect of foreign policy is essential. It is also easy. It is the easiest part
of the business. The difficult part comes not in figuring out
what one would do if one could do everything one may
wish to do. It comes in deciding what to do in the circumstances of being able to do only part of what one may wish

to do. That is the task of handling dilemmas and of rationing means. Here the making of foreign policy reaches the vital level. Here success is courted. Here failure is risked.

From this concept of the making of foreign policy as essentially involving not the mere conceiving of ends but the establishment of purposes of action and the allocation of means comes a recognition of the determinative importance of means. We know this well in the frame of individual lives. Probably not one of all the men in Sing Sing set Sing Sing as his goal in life. They all arrived there because of grievous errors in the calculation of means.

Let us then apply to foreign policy a few simple ideas relating to the economy of means.

The nation's ends, as I have used the term here, in their whole range inevitably exceed the means. It is important—nay, necessary—to maintain balance between those portions of ends chosen as purposes for action and the means available. The necessary balance between purposes and means is not solely a quantitative matter. The means must be not only sufficient to the purpose. They must also be qualitatively appropriate to the purpose.

Regard for this necessity of balance between means and purposes is the heart of foreign policy. Let me reinforce the point by quoting from the Gospel according to St. Luke:

> For which of you, intending to build a tower, sitteth not down first, and counteth the cost, whether he have sufficient to finish it? . . . Or what king, going to make war against another king, sitteth not down first, and consulteth whether he be able with ten thousand to meet him that cometh against him with twenty thousand? Or else, while the other is yet a great way off, he sendeth an ambassage, and desireth conditions of peace.

To approach policy without regard to the necessity of bringing purposes and means into balance courts not merely futility but the danger also of violence and tragedy. Certainly, for example, the history of German diplomacy in the time of William II demonstrates the peril inherent in attempting to substitute pronouncement for reality and in establishing purposes in excess of capabilities. Another example of the sequence of overreaching and then of catastrophe is the foreign policy of Napoleon III in France. History is replete with similar instances of governments which committed themselves overtly to undertakings which they could not fulfill but from which they could not back away and in consequence incurred war.

Once begun, the process of inflating the purposes is most difficult to stop. A government proclaims aims in excess of its means to effect them. Becoming anxious over the disparity between what it can do and what it has proclaimed, it seeks to redress the disparity by even wider assertions of aims still more stridently proclaimed. Eventually the range of assertions and the range of achievements are so obviously and widely disparate that the nation's policy faces imminent disintegration. Here the temptation to resort to coercion by threat and display of force rises, bringing on the danger of counterthreat and counterdisplay, and finally the plunge into general violence. Thus the course of proclaiming goals beyond the margins of capability provided by calculable means tends toward war. This course no nation can afford to begin. We must not presume for our nation any exemption from the penalties imposed for mistaking pronouncement for policy.

Having in mind that a purpose achieved in foreign policy may become the means for achieving a further purpose, let me state as a further point that the economy of means requires that the ends selected as purposes for action be such as, if achieved, will provide the best feasible basis in means for going on to achieve further purposes. That is to say, as far as possible a government disposing great power in the world must project its purposes so as best to progress toward its whole range of ends or, if it cannot progress, at least to minimize the setbacks.

These things can be figured only in a rough sort of calculus. No prodigious formulas are at hand—no easy or perfect ways, no free rides.

My last point relates to the costs.

The use of means involves cost. The achievement of purposes represents gain. It is easy to wish a gain. The difficult part is the envisaging of the cost. The cost aspects of a foreign policy are the aspects despite which a course of action is undertaken. The gain aspects are those because of which a course of action is undertaken.

In the balancing between these two aspects every important policy issue officially familiar to me has been also a close one. The merits in argument for and against an acceptable line of action never occur in ratios of 100 to 0 or even of 80 to 20. They tend rather to occur in the order of 55 to 45 or even 51 to 49. Even at best, the arguments against a line of action in foreign policy tend to be almost as weighty as the considerations in favor. Yet these small margins of difference constitute the distinction between success and failure and are all-important.

I did not find the issues so closely balanced in a former time when I used to write newspaper editorials about foreign policy. Then I could arrive at solutions plain as day and overwhelmingly cogent for even the most serious issues. The process usually took only about forty-five minutes. I did almost equally well with solving the great problems of policy in teaching international relations. In the line of responsibility, however, things look quite different.

Whatever his shortcomings as a philosopher, Jeremy Bentham was surely right in this: the forming of an intention includes the acceptance of the cost as well as the entertaining of the gain. One has truly resolved his will in favor of a course of action only in bringing his mind to the acceptance of those aspects despite which as well as those aspects because of which he acts.

This too applies to affairs of state in world relations.

The limits of our foreign policy are determined not alone by our inherent finiteness and not alone by our extrinsic capability but also by the degree of our steadfastness in shouldering the burdens. That, rather than the righteousness of unexecuted wishes, will be the test of us as a great nation. To forget this would be to say a long farewell to all our greatness.

II

Long, too long America,
Traveling roads all even and peaceful you learn'd from joys and
  prosperity only,
But now, ah now, to learn from
  crises of anguish, advancing,
  grappling with direst fate and
  recoiling not,
And now to conceive and show to
  the world what your children
  en-masse really are . . .

—WALT WHITMAN, *Drum Taps*

The Course of
the Past

I recently read a magazine article recounting the author's observations in Ethiopia. He thought it odd of the Ethiopians to regard their homeland as the focal point of world affairs. No doubt they thought it equally odd of him to think otherwise.

Any people inveterately thinks of its own domain as the center of the world's concerns and regards others, remote from that center, as outlanders. In the sense of having its own exclusive coordinates for viewing time and space, every nation gets the feeling of being a chosen people. As peoples we all tend to be like the subdebutante character in some of Mary Roberts Rinehart's stories, the one who measured the importance of contemporary events in terms of how well they could be adapted to her diary. Individuals may become cosmopolitan. Nations do not. No people ever succeeds completely in interchanging points of view with another. Each people has its own traditions. These may become familiar to others. No other can acquire the same perspectives for viewing them.

The tendency to particularism among nations, while a stumbling block to rationally contrived schemes for a perfect and universal solution of the problems of international order and peace, is by no means a wholly deplorable quality. It distresses the organizers of Utopia. Yet the same characteristic supplies the cohesiveness that enables peoples to stand against tyranny. We have seen it in our own time sustain the British in standing alone after Dunkirk. The nationalism of the occupied countries buttressed them against the German conqueror as it now strengthens them in hope against the Russian.

In the current phase of international affairs the reigning clichés and formulas reflect an obsession to discount national individuality. Supranationalism is the watchword. Rare is the statesman who does not have a plan for some other nations, if not also his own, to pool something or other and to act as if they were one instead of several. In such a time a word on behalf of national individuality may not be amiss. At the same time let us take care not to exaggerate its virtues into vice.

This latter thing happens when men seek to discover universal significance in the particular characteristics of the nations with which they are identified. In a current book Aubrey Menen discusses this tendency. He notes the quest of men of all nations "for the convincing explanation of their own astonishing excellence," adding that "they have frequently found what they were looking for." Some have found it in the theory of natural selection. Others have traced the vaunted excellence of particular nations to the will of God or to the forces of history. Those who rule in Russia trace it to a theory of reality in which their own nation is represented as the exponent of an inevitable future.

We Americans should be aware that we too are not

spared the temptation to translate our individual characteristics into universals.

For example, a contemporary author of great repute,
writing recently on foreign affairs, put forth the notion of
the American as being the first to transcend the limits of
particularism—the first, in his fancy phrase, to develop a
"planetary mind." This is merely a conceit. We are like
all the others in being ourselves unlike all the rest, and our
peculiar characteristic is not that of being universal men
among others who are more particularists.

This assumption of having planetary minds, of being a
nation peculiarly endowed with universal merits, involves
a paradox and some dangers. The paradox is one inherent
in all attitudes endowing peculiar characteristics with universal import. Such an attitude involves on the one hand
an exclusion of all others—the arrogant business of standing separately from others not graced with the peculiar virtue, whatever it may be. On the other hand, it involves the
equally arrogant presumption of seeing oneself as repre-
sentative of all others.

Let us assume neither that foreigners are peoples totally
apart nor that they are would-be Americans who happen
to wear beards. With this proportion we can go on trying
to communicate with others without feeling chagrin and
pique at failures of our friends abroad to share our premises and conclusions immediately and wholly even when
we feel so right.

Let us try to understand the distinguishing circumstances
of our past and their effects on our present outlook upon
the world. Let us do this not for the purpose of posing as
men of distinction but for the purpose of recognizing the
differences to be overcome in communicating with peoples
in the vast external realm.

The American nation is in an essential way a product
—and, one may say without undue boasting, in some
ways the most successful product—of a great movement of

peoples, culture, and power out of Europe and into areas across the seas, beginning roughly four hundred and fifty years ago.

The results of that movement have varied widely area by area as determined by a number of factors. Let us name some of the important ones and recall their application in the American experience. We shall see in sum that the combination of factors was singularly favorable with respect to the emergence of the United States—a circumstance justifying our gratitude to Providence for a windfall rather than self-admiration for our merits.

One factor is the degree of the disposition or the ability of those in authority in the homeland to keep leading strings on the overseas outpost.

At the outset the burdens of overseas interference with the British colonists in America were minimal. The colonists were left on their own. In time the homeland government attempted to attach leading strings. The attempt came too late. Its result was only to impel the American colonists to cut the lines of allegiance so as to preserve an independence already established in their hearts.

A second main consideration is the character of the political institutions translated from overseas.

The institutions implanted here from abroad were those of free individuals. They regarded government as their instrument and not themselves as the instrument of government.

The early Americans did not invent this concept. Its antecedents were developed in the Old World and translated here. They had emerged not as intellectual ideas but as the products of hard conflict.

The concepts of a freedom accessible to every man and of government as the accountable servant of a people had been known in classic times, but the lineage was not unbroken. The concepts revived as political standards in consequence of wars—the English invasion of France, the

Spanish war of liberation from the Moors, and the Italian resistance to the Holy Roman Empire. The struggle for supremacy between church and state also contributed the idea of liberty. As Lord Acton has told us, "the aim of both contending parties was absolute authority," and "although liberty was not the end for which they strove, it was the means by which the temporal and spiritual power called the nations to their aid."

The Americans received these concepts as the largess of history. The nation was spared the pain of the struggles which had produced them. Destiny enabled the Americans to make a clean start in an open land with the concepts of limited government and liberty hammered out in centuries of ordeal.

We too often forget this. We too often regard our historic opportunity not as our special fortune but as a special grace. We find it too easy to identify as our own inventions the ideas which were only given to us to embellish after others had brought them forth in struggle. We incline too much to assume concord rather than conflict as the condition of liberty. It comes too easy to us to believe that all that is needed for others to match our achievements is to make a fresh start. We tend to forget that the opportunity for a fresh start was peculiar to us.

A related factor pertains to the resources for political leadership.

Here again America was richly blessed. The leaders of the generation which achieved nationhood were men not only endowed with courage and energy but also versed in public law. They had learned from Locke, Harrington, and Montesquieu and many others the wisdom of politics at its highest sense developed over the centuries of European experience. This wisdom they adapted into American forms as the principles underlying our independence and our constitutional structure. We owe much to the circumstance that among the founders were men of ranging mind, men who read deeply, reasoned scrupulously, wrote well, and respected the intellectual function.

Let us consider also some of the material advantages in the American endowment.

With respect to the general geographic situation, embracing the accessibility, the contours, the climate, and the value of the natural resources of the overseas areas, nature favored the Americans.

While not so remote as to impede commerce and restrict the flow of objects and ideas of culture and the influx of immigrants, the position was far enough away to avoid immediate and heavy pressures from the powers in other continents. British sea power, moreover, was interposed in the intervening spaces. This provided added protection for the new-fledged and growing nation—a favorable circumstance whose importance most Americans were loath to recognize, though it was apparent to the more reflective of their leaders.

Now, with real dangers pressing from so many quarters, it is quite beyond our imagination to comprehend the way of looking at the problem of national security in world affairs under the enchantment lent by distance—and by the protective shield of British sea power—in earlier phases of national development.

In the moment of victory for independence in 1783 the Continental Congress immediately reduced the army to a strength of eighty privates, who served as watchmen over stores of military supplies at Fort Pitt and West Point. The Continental Congress simultaneously solved—or thought it solved—the problem of American naval power by simply omitting to appropriate money to maintain the handful of fighting ships then composing the Continental navy.

Marauding tribes soon forced the restoration of the army as a combat element. By the time of the establishment of the Constitution, the necessities of Western frontier security had increased the number to more than five hundred.

A half-century elapsed before the requirements of the expanding frontier had forced the figure into five digits. Piratical depredations in the Mediterranean also soon compelled the reconstitution of our navy. More than a century was then to pass before the navy's role came to be conceived of as something more than that of harrying the occasional harriers of American commerce—as an integral and pervading factor of national greatness.

The self-confidence of the early Americans regarding the national security was reflected in Abraham Lincoln's assertion of 1837—so soon forgotten were the experiences of the war of 1812—of the impregnability of the national domain even "in a trial of a thousand years" with the entire military potential of Europe, Asia, and Africa, marshaled by a Napoleon and supported by all the wealth of those continents. This was an expression not of a self-assurance peculiar to Lincoln but of something generally taken for granted by Americans. Let us remember that only four decades ago a President directed the abolition of the army's staff division for war plans on the grounds of its superfluity in view of the manifest circumstances that involvement in wars was never to be an element of national policy.

Such high expectations of a gentle destiny, such belief in a providential exemption from the vicissitudes of power, are explainable as the consequences not only of geographic circumstance but also in part of a general preoccupation with filling the boots of nationhood, as in the present and under quite different circumstances, the same views are manifested by peoples new to independence, for example our friends in India.

The new land then lying on the vast American horizon offered opportunity rather than bounty. The continental range was well forested. It was richly endowed in soil in broad and accessible expanses. It offered a proliferation of natural wealth under the surface. It had natural waterways without equal. Yet it was a land of potential to be developed, not one offering effortless enjoyment. D. W. Brogan closes one of his books with a story of an immigrant outside the Grand Central Station in New York. He was asked what forty years of experiencing life in America had taught him. He replied reflectively, "There is no free lunch." Men had to work and to earn. The opportunity lay in free land in abundance—a continent of unencumbered, unvested wealth, constituting a dowry of incalculable value for institutions, and justifying Lincoln's boast about the nation's "peaceful possession of the finest portion of the earth as regards extent of territory, fertility of soil, and salubrity of climate."

Another related factor pertains to the character of the indigenous population—its numbers, its attitude, and the strength of its culture.

The aboriginal population in that part of North America now the United States presented no grave difficulties to the expansion and enrichment of the political society and the cultures transplanted across the Atlantic and modified into American forms.

In general the tribes retreated before the oncoming pioneers. In the course of some three dozen frontier wars they were deprived of their access to the limitless open spaces and suffered as well as inflicted considerable loss of lives. Their hostility, always latent, was only sporadic. The outbreaks of violence, while marked by ruthlessness on both sides, were localized. Little by little resistance diminished. By sixty years ago it had vanished. The once-roaming tribes were settled into scattered enclaves as wards of the government.

The tribes were sparse. Their culture was simple. Their social and political forms were rudimentary. In perspective, the relations between them and the bearers of American civilization were only a minor factor.

Suppose the numbers, the cohesiveness, and the level of

attainment of the tribes had been greater. Then we—I mean our antecedents—would have had the problems inherent in imposing one culture on another and establishing a relationship of superior and subordinate between two coexisting groups of a divided society. The American venture would inescapably have been an imperial venture, and the colonists and their successors would have been cast in the role of lordship rather than that of free citizens in an equalitarian society.

As a final factor bearing on the American success story, let us take account of the circumstances of world politics in the phase of the founding and the continental expansion of the United States.

Notwithstanding our reluctance to make such admissions on the Fourth of July, let us recognize here the essentiality of foreign assistance and a resourceful diplomacy, besides American feats at arms, in the success of the American bid for independence. Our diplomacy made the most of the opportunities of world politics, first by winning the support of sovereign enemies of the Crown for American independence and second by cutting loose from them to win the Crown's recognition of independence in a separate peace.

The new United States was the world's ugly duckling. In Europe the newcomer among nations was regarded at best with indifference and in general with cold hostility. The ruling classes of Europe assumed the early failure of the United States to be a certainty and devoutly wished the hastening of it. Even our benefactors in the war of the American Revolution did not wish us well in independence.

Withal, the nation survived, expanded, and strengthened its institutions. In retrospection the historic success of the new nation appears to exceed the possibilities of conscious planning. The record seems to bear out the concept of serendipity, a word deriving from Serendip, an ancient term for Ceylon. Literature preserves its memory in a fairy tale about three princes of Serendip. They were the special favorites of benign fortune. Things never worked out as the princes planned them, but they always worked out remarkably well, nevertheless, and the princes went through life blessed with unintended and unforeseen happy consequences.

Combined with the factor of distance, the distribution of power in world relations among several nations of great magnitude—something quite beyond the capacity of the Americans to plan or to ordain—was the shielding circumstance making possible the great movement of the Americans out from their Atlantic beachhead and across the continent.

The dispersion of power only half explains, however, the insulation enjoyed by the Americans in the period of expansion. The other half of the explanation we can find in their reciprocal determination to go it alone, to avoid involvements that could only impede their penetration of the continent—a determination in keeping with Washington's farewell advice to avoid alliances until the maturing of the nation's institutions should be completed.

That dispersion of power in the Old World, combined with a determination of the Americans to go the course alone, was reflected in the historic attitude—given in the course of time the name of the Monroe Doctrine—marking out the American hemisphere as a zone of immunity against colonial penetration and interdicting the reconquest of the areas to the south where political independence from metropolitan Europe had been established.

That prudent determination to stand aloof was an essential condition for a series of successes in foreign negotiation never surpassed and perhaps never equaled by any state in a like period. Diplomacy opened the way for the filling in of the continental position. One needs only to recall the main points of the series of notable successes: the Jay

Treaty, the Louisiana Purchase, the Florida Annexation, the acquisition—if that word does not give umbrage to the citizens of that most sovereign state—of Texas; the Oregon boundary settlement, the Treaty of Guadalupe Hidalgo, the Gadsden Purchase, the annexation of Alaska, and the establishment of exclusive American rights in an isthmian canal.

This old habit of aloofness from the political concerns of the old continent was essential in its time also to the growth of the American nation not only in the territorial aspect but also in the sense of the integration into the national base of peoples and cultures of widening variety.

The nation was founded by a generation born and brought to maturity as subjects of the British Crown. The inhabitants of lands it came soon to encompass traced their antecedents to Spain and to France.

The expansion invited, and indeed required, an inthronging from Southern, Eastern, Northern, Central, and Western Europe and the British Isles. This brought an increment not alone of numbers, for in training to responsibility many millions of individuals before they moved on across the sea to enrich America with their talents, the European societies made one of their greatest contributions to the growth of our national life. Emma Lazarus' lines on the Statue of Liberty, referring to the immigrants from Europe as "wretched refuse from your teeming shore," may have edified those earlier on the scene, but they do less than justice to history in implying a unilateral bounty.

A specially relevant characteristic of the great immigration of the nineteenth century is pointed out in Oscar Handlin's book, *The Uprooted*. "The experience of these men on the move," he writes, "was more complex than that of the eighteenth-century Negroes or of seventeenth-century Englishmen or of eleventh-century Normans." Those earlier mass migrants "had either wandered to unoccupied places, where they had only to adjust to new conditions of physical environment, or they had gone under the well-defined conditions of conquering invader or imported slave." Those entering American life in the nineteenth century came into an established society "at a status equal to that of the older residents," and in relation to the law and the formal institutions of the nation "were one with those long settled in the New World." As Handlin points out, they could not impose their ways on American society and were not constrained to conform to ways already established. They faced "the enormous compulsion of working out new relationships, new meanings to their lives, often under harsh and hostile circumstances."

For the nation to have attempted taking sides in foreign issues before the new territories had been assimilated and the increments from abroad had been transformed in the alembic of America would have been incompatible with the needs of national growth.

Isolation has become a charged word, with meanings of default in wider responsibilities and of obscurantism in outlook. Yet we must see the traditions of isolation in historic proportions. It was the logical and prudent condition of United States foreign relations in the epoch of creating a nation from a potpourri of ethnic origins and filling out a continental range, and represented a realistic appreciation of the conditions of power during those decades. Of the period of isolation I can only sum up with words of a song popular in my youth, "Wasn't it wonderful while it lasted?"

Some sixty years ago Lord Bryce wrote of our country: "America lives in a world of peace. Safe from attack, safe even from menace, she hears from afar the warring cries of European nations and faiths. For the present at least—it may not always be so—America sails upon a summer sea." This was in his notable book, *The American Commonwealth*. In a later edition dated 1914—a significant year—he wrote:

"There is a part of the Atlantic where the westward-speeding steam-vessel always expects to encounter fogs. On the fourth or fifth day of the voyage while still in bright sunlight, one sees at a distance a long, low, dark gray line across the bows, and is told that this is the first of the fog banks that have to be traversed. Presently the vessel is upon the cloud, and rushes into its chilling embrace, not knowing what perils of icebergs may be shrouded within its encompassing gloom.

"So America, in her swift onward progress, sees, looming on the horizon and now no longer distant, a time of mists and shadows, wherein dangers may be concealed whose form and magnitude she can scarcely yet conjecture. . . ."

Lord Bryce misidentified the character of the cloud bank. He divined the trouble storing up for the United States to be in the nature of a deterioration in domestic economic conditions. It turned out rather to involve a radical shifting of the conditions of world politics and power. Within the dimensions of a thumbnail, with all the attendant risks of oversimplification, let us recount the salient aspects and episodes of this process.

Let us take account of the closure of the world's frontiers a little more than a half-century ago.

A consequence was the intensification of colonial rivalries.

A roughly simultaneous development was the intensification of ethnic nationalism abroad.

A consequence of this was the weakening of old multilingual empires such as the Turkish, the Austro-Hungarian, and the Russian. A collateral effect was the giving of new drive and significance to unilingual entities such as Japan and Germany.

Japan was successful in challenging Russian power at sea and in East Asia a half-century ago in the Russo-Japanese War.

The moving of the economic center in Europe northward to the Rhine and the Ruhr valleys in consequence of modern industrialization based on ferrous metals brought Germany's rise to a position of maritime and imperial rivalry with Great Britain and of preponderance over France.

The outbreak of general war in 1914 came in consequence of the rivalry over territories of the disintegrating Turkish empire between imperial Russia and Austria, both of them seeking accretions of strength to compensate for domestic feebleness, and in consequence of the rivalry between Great Britain and Germany for maritime and colonial supremacy.

Germany made an overweening bid for total victory in that war, with the consequence of bringing the United States into the array of powers against her.

The disintegration of the Austro-Hungarian empire and the finishing off of the Turkish empire came in the course of that war.

The collapse and then the bolshevization of Russia also were brought about in the course of hostilities.

The counterthrust for a decisive conclusion by the Western Allies brought the forms of victory but left Britain and France depleted in resources and man power, Italy brooding in disappointed ambition, Germany defeated but unreconciled to defeat, Russia transformed into a power base for revolutionary communism, and Japan aggrandized.

Germany returned to self-aggrandizement and violence —this time in company with Italy and Japan—and brought on a renewal of general war after a twenty-year truce. Again the United States was drawn into hostilities.

The eclipse in defeat of Germany and Japan was one consequence of this second world war.

A second consequence was the enormous widening of the power base of communism, with the westward movement of Russian armies into Eastern and Central Europe incident to the collapse of Germany and the capture of power in China by the Communists.

The war also resulted in a quickening depletion of man power and economic strength among other powers, notably the United Kingdom and France.

The further sundering of old colonial and imperial patterns was both a cause and an effect of the decline of some of the Western nations.

Two states emerged into positions of the primary scope and strength of world powers—the Soviet Union and the United States.

The lethal efficiency of warfare was drastically increased in these turbulent decades. This embraced a vast growth in the destructive force of weapons and in the radius and stealth of attack, adding new magnitudes to war.

Such were the developments marking the decline and passing of the conditions in which we enjoyed isolation. Some of the ideas characteristic of our earlier phases linger, however, though the facts have shifted.

Part of our inheritance has been an oversimplified distinction between the bad Old World and the good New World. This idea, implicit in Washington's Farewell Address and explicit in the Monroe Doctrine, goes along with the idea of confining our interests and concerns to the Western Hemisphere. For well over a century and a half Americans spoke of the Western Hemisphere as *this* hemisphere. Even presidents and secretaries of state still display the habit.

The whole world is in the American hemisphere. Any schoolboy conversant with solid geometry knows the impossibility of locating two points on the same sphere more than one hundred and eighty degrees apart. The whole world is in the same half as we are in.

Akin to the dichotomy between the bad old hemisphere and the good new one has been a suspicion of diplomacy. To many American minds it tends still to represent something of Old World shadiness and intrigue—indirect, sinister, and recondite.

Here let me digress to play with a word.

Doubleness is inherent in the word *diplomacy*. It is a relatively new English word—newer, that is, than our Constitution—coined, I believe, by Edmund Burke in 1796. Its root is an ancient Latin term for a double piece of parchment, something official written in duplicate, with the copy taken beyond the realm of origin to be explained and negotiated about with others by an emissary. The word itself implies the requirement of two—at least two—to make a bargain. It conveys the idea that more than a single pattern of interests always enters into international affairs. This sense of doubleness makes the word cognate with other terms of that essence, such as *dilemma,* with which every important policy question is charged, and *doubt,* that reservation from absolute surety always involved when unfixed factors interact.

Diplomacy often involves communication across divergences of culture, viewpoint, and interest. Attempts to edge diversity toward agreement often necessarily involve verbal complexity. Diplomacy has in some measure to have a style of its own. It is often quite essential and legitimate in diplomacy to call a spade by a synonym. This characteristic tends to give diplomatic communication, particularly to the unpracticed ear, a reputation for double-talk—a term whose invidious meaning is illustrated by a story of a man who suffered recurring social embarrassment because of the fact of his father's having died on the gallows and who in time became a diplomat and learned to cover up his embarrassment by replying to inquiries about his father: "The old gentleman suffered a lamentable death in consequence of injuries sustained in a fall caused by the collapse of the floor of a platform during a public function in which he had an important part."

Because of this aspect diplomacy took on in many American minds, to a degree beyond the warrant of fact, a character of purposeful evasion and obscuration—a color of duplicity, double-dealing, dubiousness, and deceit.

This suspicion has not been a monopoly of opponents of world cooperation. For example, even Woodrow Wilson shared it. In accepting the necessity of constant participation in world affairs, he inveighed against diplomacy, even against that diplomacy underlying the pattern of a century of general peace after Waterloo. He insisted on world assemblies as a substitute for quiet negotiation and on maxims of morality as a substitute for the restless equations of power.

A facet of the fear of diplomacy has been the lingering tradition of American ineptitude in its pursuits. In a favorite phrase of Will Rogers, the United States never lost a war and never won a conference. This carried the self-appreciating picture of a nation mighty in battle but inept in deals and subtleties.

This was not entirely true.

If the United States did not lose the War of 1812, it certainly did not win it either. That it came off lightly in the peace treaty at Ghent was due to the circumstances of international politics as reflected in diplomacy rather than a consequence of the military situation. So, discounting the military shortcomings in that war, the Americans came to maturity without having, in Whitman's phrase, to "learn to chant the cold dirges of the baffled and sullen hymns of defeat."

Besides a generally good record at arms, moreover, the Americans had also enjoyed unexampled success in negotiation. Independence and the whole westward course had been a triumph of diplomacy. It seems to me that historically we have been actually more successful in plying the technics of diplomacy and have done less favorably in the use of substitute modes for dealing with other nations.

Certainly one aspect of the suspicion of diplomacy has

been a consciousness of its essential character as a method of compromise rather than of having one's way invariably and completely.

The notion that perfection was for the asking and that anything less than perfection was failure in international dealings appeared at the outset of our experience as a nation.

For example, few would question today the prudence and the wisdom of the treaty negotiated by John Jay with Great Britain in 1794 to liquidate the problems residual from the war for independence. Few today would find its terms disproportionate to the power realities between the new and necessitous America and the rich, proud nation which it importuned. Yet contemporary critics of the treaty turned on George Washington, its sponsor, as if he were "a mad dog," applying to him "exaggerated and indecent terms that scarcely could be applied to a Nero . . . or a common pickpocket." The colorful terms are not mine but Washington's, and he was not one to indulge in self-dramatization. As the negotiator, Jay was roundly cursed as a traitor and hanged in effigy. Some nameless American wrote his sentiments on a fence, "Damn John Jay! Damn every one that won't damn John Jay! Damn every one that won't put lights in his windows and sit up all night damning John Jay!" He only expressed a general dismay at the idea of the nation's not prevailing in everything.

Americans have traditionally wanted perfection to be par for the course, and a foreign policy conceived in terms of good principles destined for inevitable triumph over evil has seemed to have more appeal to them than a foreign policy expressed in terms of interests susceptible of compromise with interests of others.

Related feelings have been the inveterate indifference to and self-righteousness about the problems of power and its component of force. The balance of power—that fortunate circumstance of world politics affording the new nation opportunity for growth into pre-eminence—became in the American lexicon something profoundly malign. For example, two decades ago the editors of the *Encyclopedia of the Social Sciences* included in it a reference to "the fantastic 'balance of power' which has been the evil dream of diplomatists since the Renaissance."

Only by giving heed to the fortuities of our position and the conditions of world politics in our historic past, conditions sparing us the necessity of having to do much thinking about world affairs, can one account for the Americans' habit of repugnance for power politics—as if there were any other kind; as if some evil inhered in giving heed in policy to the capability for achieving intended results, for such is the essence of power.

Our own institutions were rooted in political values born of centuries of conflict across the Atlantic. In our own domestic experience the contradiction of the existence of slavery within an otherwise free society had been resolved only by the sword. The nation almost died of self-inflicted wounds in the ordeal. Time healed the injury. The nation was hardly deterred in its expansive course. The Civil War came to take on the color of an aberration. The significance of the resolution by violence of the highest constitutional crisis in our development faded from memory.

Disregarding the real bearing of the factors of power and force in our own development, Americans took on the habit of assuming an inherent harmony of interest among the nations. War was regarded as the product of bad men and evil passions. Remove the bad men and apply correctives, and peace and concord would automatically result. So went the reasoning.

Reinhold Niebuhr has written with great insight on.this aspect· of our heritage and its effect on us. In his words, "America's moral and spiritual success in relating itself creatively to a world community requires, not so much a guard against the gross vices, about which the idealists warn us, as a reorientation of the whole structure of our idealism." He describes that idealism as being "too certain that there is a straight path toward the goal of human happiness; too confident of the wisdom and idealism which prompt men and nations toward that goal; and too blind to the curious compounds of good and evil in which the actions of the best men and nations abound."

Finally, our national experience has been such as to root in our minds an excess of confidence in the political efficacy of documents—in the capability of statesmen to resolve the future by agreement on the written word.

Our constitutional fathers did lay down a scheme of government. It did work. A polity grew on a foundation of stately prose. Force had been necessary to resolve the basic issues of union, but the resort to violence came in retrospect to seem an interlude and an irrelevancy. Projecting the apparent lesson of this experiment to the world of nations, Americans generally came to a disposition, a habit still in evidence, of ascribing huge importance and effect to formalized schemes and plighted undertakings between governments and to international organization *per se*.

In this manner of thinking, the simple way to concord is to arrive at agreement on paper, and the way to control the future is to have a conclave set it all down in a resolution.

Much was overlooked in the assumption that what seemed to have been the American experience would have validity for the world. The American political success was not the product merely of a document. Not sheer will alone but also a confluence of fortunate circumstances unique in the experience of nations went into the making of that success. It is easy to assume or to wish these circumstances for the world at large, but no one knows how to realize them.

We are having to relearn our lessons in one of the bitterest and most baffling phases of history ever encountered by any people. That has been the special mission and the special burden of this generation.

Besides much that has had to be unlearned, however, our development in isolation brought us much else.

It thrust us forward as the first colonial people to achieve independence and greatness as a nation and the only one to rise to the status of a world power.

It brought us a position matchless among all the great powers—a position ranging on the two greatest oceans of strategy and commerce, the Atlantic and the Pacific; spanning from the tropics to the Arctic; and lying both in the Northern and in the Western hemispheres, the two great areas of land mass and population. .

It brought us an unmatched level of technological development and an agricultural and industrial base of surpassing productivity.

It gave us an open society with strong foundations in political institutions based on the consent of the governed and the accountability of government.

These things determine our role in this mid-century. The trials of our time and the burdens and obligations imposed on us are not the wage of weakness and failure but the responsibilities of success and greatness.

Jefferson foresaw all this. Writing to John Adams in 1816, he said, "We are destined to be a barrier against the returns of ignorance and barbarism." He foretold a time when "Old Europe will have to lean on our shoulders, and to hobble along at our side . . . as she can." Of our continental position he said, "What a stand will it secure as a ralliance for the reason and freedom of the globe!"

Whitman too foresaw it:

> Thou holdest not the venture of thyself alone,
>   not of the Western Continent alone,
> Earth's *résumé* entire floats on thy keel O ship,
>   is steadied by thy spars,

With thee Time voyages in trust, the antecedent
    nations sink or swim with thee,
With all their ancient struggles, martyrs, heroes,
    epics, wars, thou bear'st the other conti-
    nents,
Theirs, theirs as much as thine, the destination-
    port triumphant. . . .

III

To achieve its objective, America
relies on personal interest, and
gives full reign to the strength
and reason of the individual.
Russia centers all authority of
society in a single man. The
principal instrument of the former
is freedom, of the latter slavery.

Their points of departure are
different, they follow different
paths. Nonetheless, each of them
seems intended through some secret
design of Providence to hold in its
hands the destinies of half the world.

—ALEXIS DE TOCQUEVILLE,
Democracy in America

The Test of
the Present

The opening words of a familiar hymn might well have
been written to describe the present situation of the United
States:

> We are living, we are dwelling
> In a grand and awful time.

Indeed, it is a time altogether too grand and too awful for
many tastes. The burdens imposed by its problems seem
greater than any nation should be called upon to bear. Its
dangers give rise to anxieties destructive of peace of mind.

Most Americans believe in inherent progress. Even the
pessimists within our culture have shared Woodrow Wilson's confidence in the "slow, painful struggle forward, forward, up, up, a little at a time, along the entire incline,
the interminable way." The more sanguine, their view of
life reflecting among other things the thought patterns of
American advertising, reject the idea of the inherent pain-
fulness of the struggle and the slowness of the progression.

Among a people so generally inclined toward the rationalist assumption of a natural right ordering of human affairs, the glaring failure of the present to fulfill the assumed tidy designs of history seems explainable only as the fault of specific and discoverable perverse or muddle-headed human acts.

This sort of thinking leads to oversimplified explanations of our troubles, with all our woes ascribed to Yalta, to Versailles, to Munich, or to some other one occasion, usually without any but the haziest knowledge of the event itself and invariably with the assumption that, but for the one occurrence in question, the present path would be without thorns or pitfalls, the tax burden light, the budget in balance, and the future secure.

One can neither prove nor deny such unitary explanations. It is impossible to reconstruct history by hypothesis. One can never say for sure in the field of foreign relations what would have happened if the things that happened had not happened. Human affairs in the larger range permit no opportunity for repeating experiences under controlled conditions like laboratory experiments so as to enable us to answer the question how different would things have been if they had been different.

The general character of the times, irrespective of particular events, is such as to make this a forbidding and difficult juncture. Moreover, its peculiar difficulties are linked to what is known as progress, or at least what is interpreted as progress in the age of the masses.

It is an age of the masses, first of all, in the simple sense of there being more and more people around, teeming in greater and greater urban concentrations.

It is an age of mass production. Mass production gives us the feasible material richness of modern life. It provides also the conditions of exaggerated interaction and the sensitivity among the various aspects of economic life within nations and between one nation and another in the scheme of international economic arrangements. Mass production reflects itself also in modern methods of central control, and the paper-work technics of recording, indexing, and disseminating—technics adapted from modern industry to the uses of political organization to make the modern totalitarian state possible.

Because this is an age of mass production, it is also an age of mass destruction. The scope and destructiveness of modern weapons are the product of—and under the logic of war an essential accompaniment of—the conditions and technics of industrial progress.

All warfare inheres in the transmission of energy and the release of it in such a way and at such a point as to do vital harm to an adversary so as to impinge on his capacity to do the same thing in return. The vastly greater concentrations of energy in weapons and the capacity to transmit them farther and with greater stealth and suddenness than in former epochs are a product of modern industrial organization. That in turn is a function of the massing of people in great urban complexes. The agglomeration of people in turn provides a special vulnerability as well as a special capability of modern society in the conduct of war. With the capability of conducting warfare resting in the last analysis on the complexes of modern industry, the foundations of economic life and the labor force itself become the targets in war.

Another characteristic related to mass production is the phenomenon of mass communication.

Modern technics make possible continuous and voluminous transmission of ideas. This process goes on both laterally from one national entity to another and vertically within nations.

Every government disposing much weight in the world has some sort of a popular base to take into account. Even those—perhaps I should say especially those—most despotic and totalitarian in character and unaccountable in conduct are constrained to preserve the forms and humor the fictions of responsibility to the people and of popular participation in the resolution of will.

Foreign relations are no longer, as in earlier times, an esoteric business involving communication among small professional groups in the various foreign offices expert in the peripheral relations of sovereigns. They involve assemblies and populaces. Their communications consist no longer mainly of stately messages addressed from governments to other governments. They involve torrents of words addressed by governments to their own populations and to the populations of foreign nations and designed for the eyes and ears not merely of a few professionals but of masses of people.

A pronouncement made in one major capital may reverberate throughout the world in a day. A crisis of government in any quarter may become a matter of instant knowledge everywhere. The world tends to take on the character of a drum: agitated at any point on its surface, it resounds throughout.

Mass communication is not confined to the transmission of words. It relates also to the general conveyance of ideas. This occurs, for example, when the mass products of one culture become widely familiar to persons living in another culture, not only among those enjoying privileged positions in society but among the general run of people as well.

Mass communication of ideas from one culture to another has drawn the world more closely together. In doing so it has widened the differences. It has sharpened the clashes of cultures by awakening consciousness of disparities in well-being between peoples in relation to the lag or the advance of production technics.

With the proliferation of populations and with the greater technical facility for getting the word around, this is inevitably an age of mass ideas. It is an age abundant with the faith that mounts movements—in the words of

José Ortega y Gasset, an era in which ". . . many men . . . homesick for the herd . . . devote themselves passionately to whatever is left in them of the sheep. They want to march through life together, along the collective path, shoulder to shoulder, wool rubbing wool, and the head down. . . ."

. Masses have marched to the piping of dreamers and knaves in every epoch; but certainly no other exceeded ours, and perhaps none has equaled it, in the capacity to produce overmastering myths and to drive men with fallacious promises of escape from sober actualities.

This characteristic manifests itself not only in demonic movements like fascism and Nazism and in the power of the appeal of communism to the frustrated elements in all societies. It shows itself in the rampant, flaunting nationalisms, with their array of unrealizable goals, among some of the peoples emerging from colonial or quasi-colonial status. We do not have to look abroad, for we can see in our own land repeated signs of this malign circumstance.

Sometimes the goal is unprecedented innovation. Again it may be glorious restoration. The difference is not important. As Eric Hoffer has made clear in his book, *The True Believer,* radicals and reactionaries are more alike than different. In common they loathe reality. They regard it "as an aberration and a deformity." They seek in mass association to break through the limits and contingencies of individual responsibility and in self-righteousness to escape the humility enjoined by righteous reason. In Blaise Pascal's words:

"Man would fain be great and sees that he is little; would fain be happy and sees that he is miserable; would fain be perfect and sees that he is full of imperfections; would fain be the object of love and esteem of men, and sees that his faults merit only their aversion and contempt. The embarrassment . . . produces in him the most unjust and criminal passions imaginable, for he conceives a mortal hatred against the truth which blames him and convinces him of his faults."

The prevalence of such impulses among great numbers of persons who lack identifications which give them a sense of significance and who therefore feel superfluous in contemporary society, the technical facilities for instant communication among masses of such people, and the technics of procedure and central control translated from modern business to the field of mass political organization combine to form the potential of totalitarianism, which, in words of Carleton J. H. Hayes, is "a brand-new event in the history of Western civilization."

The inherent difficulties of our age are the culminating problems, peculiarly complex and multifarious, of three concurrent mass revolutions—the revolution in technics and production, social revolution, and the revolutionary sundering of old colonial and imperial patterns and the emergence of once subject peoples into independence. Perhaps we should call that last the revolution of nationalism.

These three great lines of revolutionary development, charged with difficulties in any case, are made enormously more troublesome and dangerous by the position, the power, and the attitude of the Soviet Union. Its emergence, concurrent with our own, into the status of a world power complicates our lives and multiplies turbulence over the globe.

The Soviet Union is generally identifiable with the state known to history as Russia. From a base in the ancient and remote Duchy of Moscow, Russia grew to great scope concurrently with the massive movement out of Western Europe and Britain into the lands beyond the seas, including America.

The Russian expansion was the most notable extension and consolidation of a land base in history. The movement was in all directions—northward to the Arctic shores, westward to the Baltic and far into Poland, southwestward across the Ukraine, southward to reach the shores of the Black Sea and almost to encompass the Caspian, and eastward through the Urals and thence across Siberia to the Pacific shores, even crossing the Behring Straits into Alaska and then bending southward to reach the soil of present California.

In relation to its spread in the American continent this expansion was a direct concern to the foreign policy of our forebears. Russian penetration along the Pacific Coast a century and a quarter ago was a factor, now almost forgotten, in calling forth the Monroe Doctrine. Eighty-five years ago Secretary of State Seward undertook to obtain a complete Russian retraction from the American hemisphere in the Alaska Purchase—an action regarded in its day as a towering folly explainable only in terms of American gullibility in the face of Old World diplomatic guile; the Congress was prevailed upon only with greatest difficulty to put up the $7,200,000 to complete the deal.

Some discerning individuals long ago foresaw eventual significance for the world in the concurrent filling out of great ranges by Russia and the United States.

Writing from Paris in June of 1840, the German poet Heinrich Heine attributed such ideas to Napoleon—an attribution not elsewhere confirmed to my knowledge. To quote Heine: "The words of Napoleon from St. Helena that in the not too far distant future the world will become an American republic or a Russian universal monarchy are a very disquieting prophecy. What a prospect!"

At about the same time the Frenchman Alexis de Tocqueville, for another example, foretold the emergence of the United States and Russia into a great historic confrontation between two antithetic concepts of individual freedom and despotism.

Henry Adams, a worrier and therefore an atypical American, brooded over Russian expansion a half-century ago. He wrote of "all Russians" as having "the single idea that

Russia must fatally roll—must, by her irresistible inertia, crush whatever stood in her way." He noted his concern lest the "vast force of inertia known as China was to be united with the huge bulk of Russia in a single mass which no amount of new force could henceforth deflect."

Generally, however, the facts of Russian growth in the historic past were outside the scope of American knowledge and interest; history was preparing a surprise.

A circumstance of this expansion was the general lack of satisfactory natural defenses within the areas encompassed by it. Overland distance, as distinct from arcifinious barriers, became the main factor of security in the Russian mind. Anxiety about its borders remains a dominant element in the consciousness of the Soviet Union.

A second characteristic to be noted was that the Russian state, growing to encompass peoples of many varieties, remained remote from the political traditions and impulses identified with the development in the Western lands of the concept of legitimacy—that is, the notion of consent as the only valid basis for political power.

The tsarist government had made some tentative advances in the usages of responsibility in the nineteenth century and especially in the brief period between the rebellion of 1905 and the coming of general war in 1914, but on balance Russia remained a citadel of despotism and obscurantism.

A brief experiment in breaking completely away from absolutism and establishing a basis for legitimate government was made, largely as a response to Western influences, in 1917 following the overthrow of the tsarist regime. In the difficulties induced by war, free parliamentary government had little chance, however, and the experiment in republican freedom was promptly overborne by a Communist conspiratorial movement.

The conspiratorial character of the Communist accession to power is of surpassing importance. Conspiracy did not simply succeed to political power; rather it superseded political power. The conspirators remained conspirators even after taking over the apparatus of the state. They have never been willing to test their hold on power by recourse to any valid procedure of consent. They rule with fear. They rule in fear, for no one else fears conspiracy so much as a conspirator.

The Communist power within the Soviet Union has been not so much a governing force as an occupying force. Those disposing power in this system have built up semblances of popular participation in government. They are only semblances. Behind a façade of plebiscites, popular elections, and parliaments convoked to hear and to cheer but not to parley, the sanction of force is brought to bear to dominate the process of suffrage and to enforce a monopoly of information and complete control over opinion.

Of the philosophic basis of this power structure we need say only little. It consists of the social, political, economic, and epistemological theories of Karl Marx as adapted mainly by the first Soviet ruler, Lenin, and secondarily by his disciple and successor, the despot Stalin. This dogma emphasizes conflict as the norm in all relationships. Under its postulates, the whole flow of history is determined by material factors. Man himself and his mind are regarded as part of the material continuum. The moral autonomy of the individual, and with it his will and his responsibility, is denied. Human history is conceived of as unfolding stage by stage toward a plateau of perfection, where mankind in the aggregate will enjoy absolute freedom and fulfillment —implacable hostility meanwhile dividing those with interests identified with one stage of developments and others having interests identified with the successive stage.

Let us take note of the strong, though specious, appeal of this body of ideas. To the mind, suspended between a dimly perceived Absolute and an imperfectly understood material life, this dogma offers satisfaction for the two main sources of tensions—the satanic drive to deny one's finiteness and the sensual drive to lose oneself in materiality. It enables the partaking individual to regard himself simultaneously as a big shot and as one of the crowd. It enables despots to go by the title of comrade.

All this is conceived in universal terms. Those ruling as exponents of this set of concepts regard themselves as the agents of a messianic mission, determined by the logic of history to be the enemies of all antecedent and different systems and destined to triumph over all others. The conspirators succeeding to power in Russia in 1917 were conspirators against not only the displaced government but also every other government in the world.

Here is a set of notions perfectly suited to the needs of a group ruling in conspiracy and requiring the fear of a hostile world as a basis for the internal oppression necessary for perpetuating an illegitimate rule. A dogma absolving its believers from all scruple, while exalting them with the sense of being the servants of man's highest destiny, provides a perfect framework for cold, inveterate brutality. It instills a righteous assurance for the commission of the most cynical deeds. It epitomizes the corruption in historical perfectionism and historical absolutes.

This bears out the profound lesson of the twenty-fifth chapter of St. Matthew: those most assured of their rightness are the malefactors, and self-righteousness and righteousness are diametric opposites. The story told in that chapter is a simple one. All the nations come to judgment. They are divided "one from another, as a shepherd divides his sheep from the goats." Those in the first category—those found to be righteous—are astonished. In incredulity they ask when they did the good things ascribed to them. They learn their righteousness consisted in unconscious right actions of a small order—done "unto one of the least." Those in the category of the damned also are astonished at the overriding of their presumption of being right. Incredulously they ask wherein they failed. Their failure is described to them in terms not of their goals but of their defects in detail—"ye did it not to one of the least."

Setting itself in hostility to the established institutions and values of other societies, and grandiloquently stressing goals at the expense of the more exacting and duller business of justice in the details, the ideology underlying the Soviet rulership appeals profoundly to groups of individuals living as nationals of other countries—twisted idealists taken in by communism's promise of an eventual absolute solution of all social problems, frustrated individuals finding in the framework of a revolutionary effort a sense of personal significance denied to them in the relationships of established society, inwardly deficient men and women compensating for their own lacks by identifying themselves with a historic absolute, some who turn to communism in the sheeplike desire for a shepherd, and a fair share of the type described in the Book of Acts as "lewd fellows of the baser sort." Such individuals organized into the Communist apparatus in other countries as embryonic governments serve the will of the central authority of the party in Moscow and thus act as political auxiliaries of the government of the Soviet Union.

The conspiracy that walks like a state functions in a dual way abroad as well as in its own domain—conducting formal relations with other states while trying to subvert their foundations just as at home it holds in captivity those whom it claims to serve. This baleful duality Shakespeare might well have had in mind in writing certain lines in *Henry IV, Part 2*:

> Upon my tongues continual slanders ride,
> The which in every language I pronounce,
> Stuffing the ears of men with false reports.
> I speak of peace while covert enmity,
> Under the smile of safety, wounds the world.

In meeting the immediate threat of Germany and Japan and their helpers in World War II, the Western powers acquiesced in the Soviet Union's military advance to the center of Europe and its extension in Asia into positions affording it control of Manchuria and Northern Korea. Moreover, Communist participation in the local resistance in the West and in the Orient added greatly to the Communist troublemaking potential in areas beyond the Soviet military scope and prepared positions for exploiting social unrest in the sequel to the ruinous military conflict.

These developments, unfortunate as they were, have led to much second guessing of history.

One form of this second guessing is to hold it to be our great error to have participated in World War II at all. Had we stayed out, so the reasoning runs, the Soviet Union would have been on the losing instead of the winning side, and the world would be free of the menace of Soviet power, position, and intransigence.

This is frivolous thinking. Had we sought deliverance from danger by any such default, we should probably be faced now instead by another menace in the organization of the resources and positions of Europe and Africa, along with Asia and the far Pacific, under the victorious Axis.

We do not have to guess now about the intentions of the Axis powers in this respect. They set them down explicitly in the Tripartite Alliance signed at Tokyo on September 27, 1940—a pattern for the conquest of the rest of the world and the beleaguerment of the United States. Had their evil plans come to success in the war, the Axis would probably have scored great inroads also in Latin America. The victors would most probably have mastered the technics of atomic and thermonuclear weapons. By now the Nazis, comfortably settled in victory, would have made great progress in their undertaking to eradicate all free will among the conquered nations and reduce them to permanent subjugation and exploitation for the greater glory and power of the depraved oligarchy in the Fatherland. We would be under virtual siege in our continent. The factors would be far more unfavorable to us than in present reality.

One can neither prove nor refute this. It is at least as plausible as—and, I believe, far more plausible than—any other conjecture about the hypothetically different situation. It is useless to argue that our enemies' success would have been prevented anyway by some inherent logic of history. The design failed of realization only by the marshaling of adequate force against it in time.

I should not wish to give a simple answer to the question whether, given the necessity of our participation in World War II, the extensions of Soviet power were avoidable.

According to the suppositions of some, only the stimulation of Axis—especially German—intransigence by the proposition of unconditional surrender put forward by President Roosevelt and Prime Minister Churchill and by the immoderate plan, later consigned to the ashheap, for the pastoralization of Germany in the sequel to hostilities prevented the war from being brought to an early military equilibrium and settled out on the basis of a reasonable capitulation short of complete defeat of the Axis powers.

As to the formula of unconditional surrender, let me say that the need for defeating Germany decisively thus to prevent the renewal of the post-World War I legend about having been bilked into surrender had great elements of plausibility. Critics should judge the formula in the perspectives of its time. Nevertheless, having said this, I shall add my misgivings about the formula of unconditional surrender, because I regard critically all attempts to reduce complexities to slogans and to substitute absolute propositions for the contingency inhering in reality. As for the idea of pastoralizing Germany, it was humbug at best.

Let us take care not to magnify the import of these things. Let us not be taken in by the easy and illusory premise that the alternative to an unsatisfactory result is by ordinance of logic and nature a satisfactory one.

The contention is that the grim and sanguinary performance for which Hitler had trained and costumed the Germans was persisted in through the final act only because of a cue from us. This rests on too flimsy a conjecture. To the end the Nazi oligarchy used torture and sudden death against the reluctant and the dissentient. This monstrous coercion kept *Götterdämmerung* going until the final curtain. No evidence in form of facts has ever been assembled to support the opposite contention that fear of unjust intention on the part of the Western adversaries kept the hapless cast on stage until the bloody ending.

As for the hypothetical possibility of a negotiated settlement on a basis short of German capitulation, one should keep in mind that the Germans had plenty of self-motivating ambition. In his book, *In the Nazi Era,* Sir Lewis Namier does a service for proper proportions on the past by pointing out that Hitler's muted domestic opponents mainly wished to insure the maintenance of Hitler's profits without the agonies and risks of protracted war.

Moreover, a great burden of argument rests on those who conjecture that only some error in detail on our part prevented a satisfactory ending. Counterconjectures are at least equally persuasive. In Namier's words:

"What mattered most was not to reproduce the situation which, at the Congress of Vienna, enabled Talleyrand to manoeuvre between the powers of the victorious Coalition. . . . Experience has shown by now what it would have meant to seek agreement with Soviet Russia in terms to be presented to the Germans. But if differences had appeared between the Western Allies and Russia, there can hardly be a doubt which side would have been best able to buy friendship and cooperation of the Germans. . . . In short, negotiations with the Germans would not have established a German bulwark against Russia but would

have re-established a Russian-German alliance, and resulted in their common domination of the Continent
under Soviet leadership."

I press this not in dogmatic assurance of its correctness.
No one should be dogmatic about conjecture. My only
point is that this applies as well to those who answer the
problems of the present by reimagining the past.

Let us take account of another line of theorizing perti-
nent to the military strategy of the war as distinguished
from its political strategy.

According to the contention of some, the Western
Allies should have foregone invading Europe across the
English Channel and instead have pre-empted the Eastern
and Central European positions from the Russians by at-
tacking the soft underbelly.

That is a misdescription applied to Europe north of the
Eastern Mediterranean by a great man who should have
known better than to use misleading metaphors. The ter-
rain there is forbiddingly difficult for amphibious operations. Distances from possible bases to points of attack and
lack of port facilities and of conduits for supply add enormous logistic impediments. The land configurations give
every benefit to defense. One needs only to review the experiences of the Allied invasion of Italy to dispel the
specious notion of missed strategic opportunity in Southeast Europe. To have attacked there rather than where we
did might well have left the Russians with the way open to
the Ruhr.

In evaluating Allied conduct of World War II, it is well
to recall the facts and moods of the time.

In our own case, we were preoccupied—I speak here both
of the public and of the government—with the idea of
minimizing the cost in American lives. The acceptance of
such a proposition forecloses a government from weighing
the cost in blood against the eventual advantages in power
in selecting among possible paths to victory.

Moreover, the notion that the Western Allies had room for maneuver in that war is a product of refractory hindsight. Our nation suffered enormous loss in naval strength on the first day of hostilities. In an ensuing period lasting into 1943 it was touch-and-go as to whether the attrition due to Atlantic submarine warfare might not eliminate us from the war effort. In the winter of 1944-45 we had committed the last of our reserves in the ground fighting in Europe. These are factors to be taken into account in testing theories as to how to have fought that war so as to come out with everything set aright. It is too easy, and too discrepant with truth, to argue now as if in the conduct of that war our side had great margins of choice and only frittered them away.

Some of the attitudes pervading the nation at that time had a bearing.

In general Americans, many of them in high places, regarded war as an aberration—an irrational interruption of the rational flow of history, something to be got over and done with as easily and rapidly as possible so as to permit events to resume their usual course.

In this mood, the nation tended to regard with indifference and unawareness the vital questions of power in the postwar world. The enormous effects of attrition, of exhaustion, and destruction in reducing the United Kingdom and France as power centers were not anticipated. The disarrangement of the world following upon the eclipse in defeat of Germany and Japan was only dimly perceived.

Basic to this faulty perception was, I believe, an inadequate habitual way of regarding the problems of power. The habit was to look on world power problems as inherently involving quantities. This is distinct from the way of regarding power implicit in Tolstoi's exposition of it as relationship between one who resolves will and others who respond thereto.

Under the quantitative view of power, the problem

caused by evil exercise of power by particular entities is solved merely by nullifying their capability. From this standpoint it seemed plausible to create the foundations of a better peace simply by depriving of power those deemed the malefactors of World War II.

The problems of power regarded as a relationship are seen in quite different terms. Under this concept, let us say for purposes of analysis, the units of power disposed among nations always add up to one hundred, whatever the degree of intensity with which they may be exercised at any moment. In a rough analogy, let us think of a pie all of which must be distributed. The degrees of circumference encompassed in all the pieces of pie, however sliced, total three hundred and sixty, no matter how thick or thin the pie may be. To deprive certain entities of the privilege of sharing in the pie necessarily requires a reallocation of pie among the still eligible recipients. In the same way, to reduce to a nullity certain repositories of power in world affairs has as a necessary consequence a wrenching readjustment among the others.

By following the quantitative rather than the relative concept we failed to see clearly enough that the power knocked from German hands would have to be taken up by others. We failed to anticipate the deadly competition bound to ensue when the forced vacating of power by Japan had transformed the power question in the Far East into one of who would pick up the pieces.

In Central Europe, Western forces, including ours, were on the scene. By the fact of territorial possession we perforce had to become the heirs of a portion of the vacated power. In Japan, too, our forces were on the scene in the islands proper. Japanese power, however, had been exercised also on the mainland of Asia. We had no intention whatsoever of stepping into the Japanese boots there. We assumed that the heirs to the power relinquished by Japan would be Chinese elements disposed to cooperate with the

West in return for Western support. It was assumed that statesmen could determine the succession to Japanese power by agreements made at far removal from the scene of issue. Here, however, was a question to be settled not so much by the will of Western statesmen as by factors and forces operative within China.

The routing of Western forces in the earlier phases of World War II in the Far East had largely eclipsed the image of the West. The support and patronage of Western powers came to take on the character of liabilities as well as of assets in the rivalry for political power on the East Asian mainland. Thus, by a paradox cruel to Western interests, a long-dreamed aim of our policy, the emergence of China as a great power, was realized—but under auspices quite other than intended.

It would be bootless for me to add my voice to the polemics over questions of personal responsibility for this unfavorable issue of events. I am interested here not in blame but in analysis. My only purpose is to point to the folly of projecting political plans with insufficient account of the irreducible realities of power.

Akin to the prevailing disregard of actualities of power was a preoccupation with the mechanics of world relations. A great many important Americans became concerned primarily with schemes for a universal international organization. Uneasy conscience was an element in this. The League of Nations had been originally an American proposition. After having fostered the League and having achieved acceptance of it by our associates in World War I, the United States had stood aloof. The League had failed to fulfill the hopes placed in it as a means of perpetuating peace. This seemed to place on American fickleness some portion of the blame for the world's tragedy. This time— so the notion went—the world should make a fresh start on international organization, with the United States getting in and staying in. A permanent concert of the great powers and a periodic town meeting of the world's governments great and small would take care of the problems of position and power and political conflict. Such was the hope.

A factor in the American approach to peace in the immediate sequel to World War II was also the assumption—due to prove so vain so soon—of a long-term monopoly on atomic capabilities as a source of strength both in military terms and for international bargaining purposes. Officials and publicists were still referring to the Manhattan Project as the best-kept secret of the war. The Western statesmen present at Potsdam at the moment of the apprising of Stalin of the brand-new development of the atomic weapon were still ascribing his lack of surprised reaction to an assumption that he had not fully understood what was being told him.

While noting this passing reliance on an assumed monopoly of atomic capabilities, I should warn against over-emphasizing this point. As a nation we are just not as calculating as that. The anticipation of a push-button peace prevailed long before the atom bomb was invented. I recall, for example, that in the campaign of 1944 the allegation—unfortunately not true—of an intention by the government to maintain military effectiveness after the close of hostilities was brought forth by the challenging candidate not in tribute to the government's prudence but as an accusation against its trustworthiness.

To the men of the Kremlin, imbued with the fears and ambitions peculiar to their outlook, the situation following upon World War II must have seemed to offer matchless historic opportunity.

The home base had suffered badly under the depredation of war, but in the tide of victory the Red Army had filled the historic buffer areas between Russia and the West and had flowed into Central Europe. In the Far East Soviet forces had taken over areas long within the range of Russia's coveting but heretofore beyond its reach. Wherever the Red Army was in control Communist rule was established and opposition put under intimidation; and in some instances, as in Yugoslavia and Northern Iran, and in some degree also Finland, the political frontiers even exceeded the military for a time.

Germany and Japan had become nullities in the equations of military power. The peoples of Western Europe were still under the moral shock of occupation and the fatigue of battle; their divisions of purposes and deficiencies of energy were reflected in a deterioration of governmental authority, and aggrandized Communist parties in Moscow's service were at hand to widen every rift, to worsen every difficulty, and to take over power when opportune. Communist armies were in the field against the government in Greece. Turkey was under acute pressure.

The bonds of control between West and East had been sundered or at best weakened, and new threads of confidence had not grown to replace them. Old grievances against the West rather than the problems of meeting new responsibilities preoccupied the Oriental peoples emerging into independence. Indigenous Communist forces were gaining the upper hand in China and laying siege to governments in Southeast Asia and the offshore countries of the South China Sea.

Vengeance toward the defeated, arrogance to the partners in victory, and obstruction and waywardness in the affairs of the United Nations emerged as the distinguishing features of Soviet policy.

No combination of nations adequate to maintain a vital basis of free collaboration and to counteract the factors of fear engendered by the Soviet Union was possible without the permanent participation of the United States. The unfolding of this circumstance in the immediate postwar years brought the United States into an entirely new relationship to the vast external realm.

This new relationship has tested profoundly and exactingly the moral strength of the nation.

Our position, our resources, and the durability of our institutions are the basis of our power. The scope of our power has made our participation essential to the preserving of the causes with which our interests lie. In this way power has become the measure not of our freedom but of our responsibility.

While losing a sense of freedom, we have lost also a sense of efficacy. In an earlier time, when we stood normally aloof, our decision to become a world factor for a season had drastic and immediate results in redressing the balance. Now that is gone. By becoming permanently involved, we are no longer vouchsafed opportunity to alter the situation dramatically and radically by sudden entrance onto the world scene.

Finally, we no longer enjoy the privilege of limited concern. Our confrontation with the Soviet Union encompasses the globe. Developments in every quadrant reflect and react in every other quadrant. Problems which in previous epochs would have been beyond our notice now preoccupy our minds and draw upon our resources.

We are having to learn for ourselves a lesson well known to history—that the greatness of nations is measured not in glory and majesty but in the capacity to carry burdens.

IV

. . . world order, in all its forms,
from peace between states to legal
documents which justify legitimate
governments, is a labor of Sisyphus
which man must always begin anew,
a structure continually undergoing
repair because it begins to disintegrate at the very moment that it is
being built. One of the greatest mis-
takes committed by human indolence is the belief that order is best
preserved by keeping it as it stands.
The only real guardians are those
who reconstruct it.

—GUGLIELMO FERRERO,
The Reconstruction of Europe

Consent and Coalition

President Washington's Farewell Address one hundred and fifty-seven years ago counseled the young nation to have "as little political connection as possible" with other nations, to regard Europe's primary interests as having at most a very remote relation to America and the causes of Europe's controversies as "essentially foreign to our concerns," to avoid "interweaving our destiny with that of any part of Europe," indeed "to steer clear of permanent alliances with any portion of the foreign world," and to suffer participation only in temporary alliances demanded by expediency, never to "quit our own to stand upon foreign ground," and to take "care always to keep ourselves by suitable establishments on a respectable defensive posture."

In recent years all but one of the items of Washington's counsel have been overturned by events.

Our forces stand on many foreign grounds. Some serve as elements in the defense of Western Europe in Germany and Austria and in lines of communication across France.

Some of our forces man bases in the United Kingdom, in Iceland, in Greenland, among countries adjoining the Mediterranean on its southern and eastern coasts, and in island areas of the Far Western Pacific. Our armies remain in South Korea in the still unresolved sequel to a vexing and enormously destructive coalition war. Others of our forces maintain the security of Japan.

We find our destiny interwoven not merely with Europe's but indeed with that of all the continents. The causes of controversies in other continents, instead of being "essentially foreign to our concerns," have become matters of pressing moment to us. They require constant effort, huge outlay of resources, and continuous collaboration with many other governments. We are daily involved in the question of the future of now divided Europe, in the efforts to maintain a basis of economic and military strength to relieve the political societies of Western Europe from anxieties and frustrations tending to make them susceptible to Soviet pressure, in the search for better bases of accommodation between the metropolitan powers and the peoples of the Middle East and the Far East new to or aspiring to independence and strange to the usages of responsibility, and in the encouragement of and assistance to a score or more of nations to stand firm against Communist pressure both from without and from within.

We have a set of alliances. They are intended not as temporary but as enduring arrangements. They are founded not upon expediency but on principles of political collaboration. Their scope is without example in previous history for any nation, compassing the entire American hemisphere, the North Atlantic area, Western Europe from the North Cape to the Mediterranean, and the Mediterranean area itself, stretching through Turkey to the eastern limits of the Black Sea, and finally embracing the Pacific. One treaty engages us in obligations of mutual defense with twenty American republics to the south of us. Another such treaty embraces Canada, the United Kingdom, Iceland, Norway, Denmark, the Netherlands, Luxembourg, Belgium, France, Portugal, Italy, Greece, and Turkey. Three concurrent alliances bind us to Australia and New Zealand, the Philippines, and Japan. Still a fourth, in formative stage, would so engage us with the Republic of Korea.

Auxiliary to these explicit alliances are mutual defensive arrangements of less formalized contractual character with Spain and Yugoslavia and with the Chinese Nationalist government at its seat on Formosa. We are intimately concerned too in the defense of Indochina. In the United Nations we are a principal among the group of nations disposed to stand free of Soviet domination. We have in the occupation of Western Germany and Austria a special coalition of responsibility with the United Kingdom and France.

This is enough for a cataloguing of our concerns and coalitions—our deviations from Washington's farewell counsel. The key to these deviations is found in the last and most important item of his advice—that about keeping a respectable defensive posture. The circumstances of this mid-century make it impossible for us to do this and to follow the other items of his counsel at the same time. We have had to reach out in a system of alliances to keep from hostile hands the control of positions and resources that would shift the balance perhaps irretrievably against us, to secure the time and the space necessary to fend off attack, and to secure the positions for insuring against encroachments on the seas by forces inimical to our interests. Our alliances are not gestures of quixoticism but actions essential to our own security. Our forces stand abroad not in the service of foreign interests but in the service of American safety.

Once upon a time two cross-eyed men collided. One asked the other why he did not look where he was going.

The second asked, "Why don't you go where you're looking?" In former times, as a nation remote from and only intermittently involved in the affairs of the Old World, we were concerned chiefly about looking where we were going. Now as a world power we must take heed that we shall go where we are looking. We must take care to understand the values which our foreign policy must serve and the manner in which they constrain the nation to proceed on the world scene.

Whatever the case in earlier times, certainly under the interactive conditions of contemporary politics a world power cannot lead a double life. It cannot espouse one set of values at home and then cheat on them in the world at large. It cannot adopt one mode of action in domestic matters and act by its antithesis beyond the threshold. Its choice of what to be within itself must determine its conduct in the world, or else its conduct in the world must transform the character of its domestic institutions.

The government of the United States is founded on some general propositions set down in the Preamble of the Constitution. These are the purposes for which the American people gave their consent to be governed.

The first is the perfection of the Union. That expresses the idea of a nation growing in internal strength and concord.

The second is the establishment of justice. That means subjection of power to antecedent standards insuring against the employment of power as an end in itself.

Third in the enumeration comes domestic tranquility—meaning a nation at peace with itself, permitting the resolution of issues by reason and compromise.

Next comes the common defense. That means the protection of the nation against penetration by its enemies.

The promotion of the general welfare is listed next. That expresses the idea of a government serving the interests of, and accountable to, the community at large rather than being the instrument merely of the interests of a dominant group.

Finally comes the securing now and henceforth of the blessings of liberty, a situation permitting the individual to choose freely for himself and his children regarding the modes of their lives, their religion, and their thoughts.

Those values prosper in a climate of security. They would wither under the blight of dread. The goal of our foreign policy, enduring until death or defeat, is to preserve in the world a situation permitting the survival of those values as political realities in the United States.

Behind these ideas in the Preamble of our Constitution is implicit the concept of a people's giving consent as a condition precedent to being governed. The Declaration of Independence states that concept explicitly in a phrase declaring the consent of the governed to be the sole source of the lawful powers of a government. The ages echo in that phrase. What it conveys is perhaps the most precious and rational idea brought forth through the centuries to rectify and to justify the exercise of political power.

Of this idea we as a nation must be advocates and exemplars in the world to fulfill the highest implications of our institutional values. Let me therefore take a few minutes to deal with it analytically.

As an initial point in analysis I refer again to the concept of intention. I used the term in an earlier discourse to denote the whole scope of a contemplated action, including the means as well as the purpose. Continuous adjustment among patterns of intention inheres in all human relations. Individuals, groups, and institutions affect the intentions of other individuals, groups, or institutions and in turn experience action upon their own intentions by others. One continually seeks to get others so to modify their undertakings as to suit one's own purposes, or on the other hand adjusts his own intentions to fit the designs of others.

A power relationship is one involving, on a continued basis, the adjustment of patterns of intention between or among various entities having wills. To bring another regularly to comply with one's own purposes is to exercise power. To accommodate one's intentions regularly to the will of another is to be acted upon by the power of another. Power, let us say, is the capacity to achieve intended results by affecting the actions of others.

In an oversimplification—a pardonable one, I trust—let me point to two general ways of affecting the intentions of another entity.

One way is to bring the other one concerned to an identification of his purposes with one's own purposes. This is the method of seeking a community of will with another. It leaves the other with the opportunity of choice, which is the condition of freedom. It involves essentially also having in some measure and on occasions to bend one's own intentions to accommodate one's counterpart in a merging of wills. Let us identify this as the method of consent.

The other way is that of impinging upon another's means so as to foreclose him from acting otherwise than in accord with one's own desires. This involves the mastery of one will over another. Just as opportunity for choice is the condition of freedom, the deprivation of another's choice is the condition of domination or coercion. This course requires rigidity of will on the part of the one disposing power, just as in the opposite case some flexibility in the fiber of the will is required.

The basic form of coercion is force. Force, as I use the term here, refers to the direct or the threatened or implicit application of energy in a violent way to compel, to constrain, or to restrain another.

The state rests on the establishment of a monopoly to the prerogative to use force in a defined area. Integral to the political organization of a people is the location of a monopoly of force in a government which alone through its agents is entitled to initiate its use or to lay down the conditions authorizing private individuals to use it. This integral relationship between the existence of the state and a monopoly to the title to use force is a concept in classic political theory. I shall merely assert it here rather than attempt to labor the point in argument.

The faculty for eliciting consent as a basis for power I shall call authority. That is not the sole meaning of the word, but it is one of its meanings, and I know of no substitute for it in this sense. By authority I mean a power based not only on capacity to compel compliance but also on trust by those who obey.

Force and authority are not antithetic. The command of adequate instruments of force by government is necessary to that protective capability in turn essential as a basis for eliciting consent. On the other hand, coercive power alone is a very brittle base on which to maintain a state. The reliance on force alone as an instrument of compliance generates anxiety among those subject to the power of the governing apparatus and among those exercising the power of the apparatus. The ruled fear the rulership. The rulers fear the ruled. Fear induces fear. The history of a hundred tyrannies demonstrates this. Even the most ruthless tyrannies covet consent and contrive a semblance of authority by propagating among the ruled slogans and symbols of esteem and affection for the rulers and fashioning façades of franchise and accountability.

The most pervasive and enduring issue of politics is one of primacy between consent and force. This is the key to the question whether the power of a government rests on real or sham authority.

An illegitimate rule is one resting solely on the monopoly of force, gaining compliance only by coercion. Despite the trappings of authority used to conceal the nakedness and singularity of the force by which they govern, those in the seats of power can never forget the oppressive character of their rulership. They will tend toward wariness and fearfulness of groups and institutions independent of the governing apparatus and capable of eliciting consent.

An illegitimate rule of the modern totalitarian variety is capable of going far, far beyond the simpler despotisms of former times, in coping with the challenges implicit in the existence of other institutions and loyalties within its domain. This enhanced capability is inherent in several circumstances. One is the character of modern electrical and electronic communications, which tend naturally to a monopoly under the regime's control and give it huge advantages over opposition in surveillance and pursuit. Another is the ostensive character and the complexity of armor and high fire capability in modern weapons—characteristics which afford a regime a monopoly of force never commanded in times of smaller and simpler arms. A third is the capacity to proliferate information and the command of virtual monopoly over the circulation of it and therefore of the power to determine what shall pass as true.

Moreover, a modern totalitarian regime, resting on a mass base, is inherently more sensitive than the former, simpler despotisms to the existence of other patterns of loyalty, for these represent possible rival attractions and therefore a potential threat to its own mass base. The tendency of such a rule is to stamp out such groups and institutions where feasible and to subsume all semblance of authority unto itself—to establish a monopoly on institutional life, to use its coercive instruments to rub out every pattern of loyalty independent of itself, in a word to manifest its totalitarian impulses.

We call such a regime totalitarian because of these impulses in it. These impulses arise out of its totalitarian character. The necessities of power drive such a regime in the direction of stamping out all rival loyalties. The opportunity to use the monopoly of force to impose uniformity of loyalty is what impels totalitarian movements to covet and to seek control of the mechanism of government. It is hard to sort out cause and effect in these matters. Let us note these characteristics as concomitants without trying to determine which causes which.

To bring out the differences between government resting on valid authority and government relying on sham authority, I cite Guglielmo Ferrero, a historian with great insight on this question:

"Bringing it down to a mere matter of force, government would be no more than a perpetual struggle between those who, considering themselves the strongest, would desire to be in control. Under these circumstances, how can a government assume its proper function as an instrument of reason and source of laws which limit and direct the unbridled independence of the human mind? . . . In order that a government may accomplish its organic function as the instrument of reason and the creator of laws, its subjects must conform jointly and spontaneously, obeying its commands voluntarily, at least to a certain extent; and they will not give their spontaneous submission unless they recognize that the government has the right to command, apart from the force necessary to impose its orders."

Man's great accomplishment in achieving decency in civil society, Ferrero has written, was ". . . when he asserted that government does not have the right to command because it is strong, but that it must have the strength to command because it has the right to do so. Strength is not the parent, but the servant of the right to command."

In the usages of legitimacy those charged with applying the sanctions of the state are denied the power independently to determine the general purposes for which the sanctions may be applied. The coercive power of the state, moreover, must be withheld from the processes of resolving the general purposes for which the use of coercive power is to be authorized.

Here in the antithesis between illegitimacy and legitimacy in use of power among nations—between coercion and consent—we find the key to the basic issue between the Soviet power on the one side and our allies and ourselves ranged on the other.

The peoples of the Soviet area are captives of rulerships. These rule with fear. They rule in fear. The ideology employed by them conduces to this result. This ideology denies and inverts the whole set of values integral to legitimacy in the exercise of political power. The Soviet regime in its present character could not enter into bonds of confidence with other regimes different in character from itself and independent of its dominance. Its domestic character forecloses it from being able to do so.

In these generalizations I have sought to avoid labored description of the connections between the Soviet Union and the European satellites and Communist China respectively. To some may occur a question whether my words are so chosen as to take into account the special relationship, more a partnership than a servitude, of the Peiping regime to Moscow. Elements of consent seem to infuse this partnership. The collaboration is one between like regimes. Each in its way seems compelled to eradicate within its own domain all impulses and loyalties to traditions and values not identified with itself. Each seems impelled by the logic of its own general beliefs and own view of its particular situation to a mission to dominate adjoining countries up to the limit of capability. Each seems drawn into collaboration with the other to add vicarious strength and advantage to itself in fear of the outside hostility implicit in its own hostility toward entities different from itself.

I shall not venture to guess as to the character of the relationship under different conditions. Given their character and outlook, the regimes in Moscow and Peiping will probably find more reasons for collaborating than otherwise in the calculable future. Insofar as the collaboration may be said to rest on consent it is a consent derived from a shared fear of and enmity for other outlooks. It is a consent resting on a common negation of consent.

Let us turn now to the part assigned to the United States. Our role must be to advocate for the principles of legitimacy in relationships with the vast external realm because that is the ground on which we must stand at home. To attempt the collaboration of fear and intimidation with other nations would necessarily involve us in the undoing of the principles of free government at home—the principles whose survival must be the pervasive and enduring goals of our foreign policy. As the adversary's design is to dominate by fear, our aspiration must be to do whatever we can to lift the burden of fear from the world so as to give free institutions and usages the best attainable chance to survive and to strengthen. Ours is—and it must continue to be—the course of consent.

Let us consider briefly the interaction between the Soviet imperium and the world exterior to it.

The interpretation of world affairs suffers because the range so vastly exceeds personal observation and experience. One is usually at a loss for precise words to convey the essence of the functions, equipoises, and contradictions making up relationships among states. To explain to oneself or to others one tends to borrow language and concepts from other fields. We interpret world affairs in analogies from the bridge table, the stock exchange, medicine, physics, and so on.

A favorite source of analogy is sports. In our national sports the contenders take turns in offense and defense, as in baseball at the half-innings and in football when the ball goes over. Perhaps this accounts for the tendency to regard the offensive and the defensive in foreign affairs as mutually exclusive. One repeatedly hears the cliché about moving from the defensive and taking the initiative, in a tone of utterance indicating the sayer's assurance of having put forth something significant and wise. The idea, however, is false and misleading. In world politics adversary powers are continuously both on the defensive and on the offensive just as in the relationships of chess, fencing, or Gaelic football.

We should probably have to go into calculus to find a satisfactory analogy. A nation's intentions and its power interact on each other. What we seek is largely determined by what we can do. What we can do is determined in part by what we are after. Our own aims and power, acting as functions of each other, are in an interactive relationship with adversary intentions and capabilities, which also are related to each other as interdependent variables.

Such characteristics of complexity make me quite wary of attempts to scan and to plan the future in nice precision. The interval ahead within which our hypotheses can have validity is limited. To carry our speculations beyond it takes us into realms of fancy. There is a story of a man who tried to board a train with a mongoose on a leash. The conductor told him pets were forbidden. The man insisted the mongoose was not strictly a pet because it was needed to kill the snakes he saw in delirium tremens. The conductor said this was unacceptable since snakes in delirium tremens were not real. The passenger said that, for that matter, it was not a real mongoose. One arrives at this sort of unreality in attempting to project very far ahead hypotheses about the interactive relationship between the Soviet sphere and the areas independent of it.

The Soviet system may be described as an arrangement for extending the span of control, yet always keeping it rigidly under the will of the central authority. It seeks to do with greater effect and imagination what the misguided program of the Nazis tried to do in exercising a claim of allegiance and obedience over citizens and subjects of other states and in trying to reverse the trend toward equality and freedom among the world's components and to extend a central imperial dominion over areas of established independence.

The primary source of the coercive element holding this system together is in the Kremlin. If this element were deprived by circumstance of its capability to dispose the power of fear throughout its system through its armed forces and the disciplined Communist apparatus, the satellite system would fall apart, and the partnership in coercive design with Communist China would be riven.

Strength and determination in the world outside present a constant challenge to the foundations of power within the Soviet system. Firm and united in the will to stay clear of Soviet domination and to resist Soviet expansion, the nations outside that system give the hope of a better day and keep alive courage among many millions in thrall to communism.

Anxiety over the challenge and competition to its own domination within its own sphere from the areas beyond its control impels the rulers within the Soviet system to press on the areas beyond—like a mythical man in Texas who bought up seven counties bit by bit because he liked to own the lot next door.

As unity and strength in the world beyond its periphery will block the Soviet from further aggrandizement, the Soviet rulers will continue constantly to bank on and to press for disunity among the outside powers. They will seek a return to the more advantageous times when the Soviet Union could turn the flank by dealing with one adversary against the interests of rival adversaries in the style of the deal with Weimar Germany against the West at Rapallo, of the simulated *rapprochement* with the West against Nazi Germany in the phase of the United Front, and of the pact with Germany against the West in 1939.

Negotiations for Soviet advantage by using one adversary against others is categorically different from negotiation with united powers. Negotiation of this latter character can succeed only in the direction of an abatement of tensions and a solution of issues—that is, toward accommodation. Negotiation of this latter direction runs counter to the idealogical view of life underlying the Soviet system and the view of the outside world logically necessary to the maintenance of the interior conditions essential to the continuance in power of the present regime as it is.

So, wishing to avoid war and yet determined to prevail, the Soviet rulers anticipate a schism among the adversaries to provide the opportunity for the Soviet Union to serve the end of its ultimate triumph.

One logically possible course for the powers ranged in opposition to Soviet encroachment is to precipitate a general war in an attempt to redress the balance with the Soviet Union in their favor by acting radically on the factors of force.

This offers unconditional assurance only of radically worsening the conditions of the world in the sequel to hostilities. In the ruin, the exhaustion, and the delinquency then prevailing, the survivors, such as they might be, would look back on present times, with all their dangers, anxieties, and frustrations, as a golden age.

A second logical possibility is, by giving consent to present divisions, to seek to settle our differences in a *modus vivendi* on a world scale.

Here again the idea is not apposite to the problem. Such a deal would not alter the character of Soviet rulership. It would merely write off to Communist domination, without contest, the strategic shortest land range between the Baltic and the Mediterranean. It would consign to Soviet domination, beyond hope of redemption as a basis for moral resistance, the populations of Communist-dominated areas in Europe and Asia. It would permanently surrender to unimpeded Soviet exploitation an area of Europe of high importance in industrial development and raw material resources. It would write off the people and the resources of China. It would strengthen the Kremlin's hold on the entire imperium and foreclose what Secretary Dulles has called "the vast possibility for peaceful change." It would magnify the Kremlin's capacity for exerting pressure beyond its periphery. It would enormously enhance the prospect of eventual Kremlin success in the world contest and thus encourage rather than hinder Communist subversion within the appeasing countries themselves.

One may suppose that, behind the concealment afforded by the freedom of Soviet power from accountability, the dilemmas confronting the rulership are exigent. The risks of playing out the course in the hope of a verification by destiny of Soviet hopes to divide the powers ranged in opposition must press on every major decision.

The best course for the powers ranged on our side appears to be to intensify that dilemma by so holding on, so husbanding strength, so discovering and developing among themselves common purposes as to compel the Kremlin to revise its expectations.

This is not a riskless course. No riskless course is available. In persevering in it, it is well to keep in mind one true element in Hegelian analysis· the point of resolution is the point of highest contradiction. The best hopes lie in creating the circumstances for a heightening of the dilemma within the Soviet framework, eventually to move it along the course of accommodation and thereby toward its own historic transformation—always with a knowledge that the pressure on the rulership to resort to general violence as a solvent may well increase as the point of crux is approached.

A modicum of unity in the areas free of Soviet domination is an essential condition of this process.

Just as the Soviet Union is the wellspring of the coercive forces binding its system, so is the United States in a central and determining position on the side of its interests. No

combination of nations adequate to deal with the factors of
fear engendered by the Soviet system is conceivable without the participation and fostering interest of the United
States. Surely the coalitions on our side would disintegrate
if we should fall short of that responsibility through internal contradictions, want of insight, failure of will, failure to take adequate measure of our tasks, or failure to
abide by Washington's still valid advice to maintain a
respectable posture for defense.

It would be vain of me to pretend to having conclusive
wisdom on the problems of relating ourselves to our friends
in the world. It would contradict one of my main points
in these discourses—to wit, the illusoriness of systematic
answers in world politics.

Surely the responsibility enjoins upon us the qualities
of magnanimity, urbanity, and patience in portions greater
than it has been our habit to show in world affairs.

It is all very well to make phrases about the unity of the
free world. Phrases about unity do not settle issues over
differences of interests. The nations more or less disposed
to side with us present a complex of differences. Their
variety and intensity are novel. So also to us is the experience of feeling concern in many international issues remote in origin and often obscure in substance to our point
of view and yet important to us for the dangers implicit in
them if they should get out of hand. We cannot expect
them soon and easily to be resolved. Neither can we afford
to let them run their course in violence. We have at least
to try to make and to keep them manageable. This is oner-
ous business both materially and morally. It requires of us
the wisdom to understand that anything worth doing at all
is worth doing imperfectly.

We must relate ourselves to our friends, moreover, not
only as arbiters and exemplars but also, in some particu-
lars, as opponents, for valid differences of view and interest
often arise between our collaborators and us. So the clash-

ing interests which we must help resolve in higher synthesis sometimes include our own interests. This requires of us the highest moral capacity of politics—the capacity to be just in one's own cause, to be as jealous of an opponent's rights as of one's own, and to suffer differences without permitting them to divide.

This attitude is as essential in relating a free nation to others that it would lead as it is in healthy domestic politics. In this respect our external and internal political situations are linked. To restless, seeking men of absolute minds the attitude of comity is repugnant in either sphere. There is no surer way of blighting freedom everywhere than by impairing the image projected by the United States to the world. There is no surer way of defeating freedom here than by clouding the nation's title to respect among its friends, for that can only serve our adversary and move the factors of security in the world against us.

The conduct of alliances and coalitions was complex and subtle enough in times when international relations was the business of personal sovereigns exercising directly or through ministers a plenary prerogative in dealing with external interests and forces. It is immeasurably more complicated and elusive in the circumstances calling on our nation to exercise leadership—a time when governments in external affairs must act responsively to domestic political forces.

In discussing international relations many still tend to reflect outworn assumptions of the continuity and the plenitude of power of governments, just as if in their foreign undertakings governments were endowed like sovereigns in earlier times. Those speaking for governments now—and I refer to free governments specifically though my observation applies in large degree also to dictatorial regimes—must be continuously aware of the fluctuating character of their agency. Their capabilities to act and to give promises of action rise and fall as functions of their horsepower in domestic politics. The forward surges in accommodation among allies are possible only in the intervals when all concerned are concurrently confident of command of domestic support.

Our power to solve the factors bearing on the capacity of friendly governments to take effective action in concert with us is small. We can at least, however, prevent feebleness on our own national account from being a retarding circumstance. As citizens we can at least develop a degree of understanding of the problems of those representing us as to permit them opportunity to show and to apply wisdom insofar as it is theirs to show.

Discussing world affairs in a letter to John Adams in 1816, Jefferson wrote: "Bigotry is the disease of ignorance, of morbid minds; enthusiasm of the free and buoyant. Education and free discussion are the antidotes of both." The case against enthusiasm—against the tendency to approach the problems of foreign policy with a billowy good feeling and an insufficiency of proportion—is just as important in its way as the case against bigotry. Indeed, they are related phenomena. Each rests on generalized self-righteousness. Moreover, the inevitable disappointment of the one approach often serves to enlarge opportunity for the other.

Let me then set forth a few general things incumbent upon us to keep in mind. Those among us in the competition of politics may well learn them along with the rest.

In a poem by Carl Sandburg a soldier-of-fortune asks the Sphinx to speak and to reveal the distilled wisdom of all the ages. The Sphinx does speak. Its words are, "Don't expect too much." That is good counsel for the nation. We should not expect of our magistrates great accomplishments without great risk, pain, and expense to ourselves. We should not take them to task for failing to realize for us such exemption from vicissitude as was illusorily assumed to be ours in the past. We should give up the silly luxury of holding them accountable for not having super-human foresight.

We should learn the complex and vexing character of the world as seen, if they are wise, by those who govern. We should not indulge ourselves in such political fantasies of perfection as tempt those in authority to humor us with unfulfillable promises. Far from applauding, we should learn to spurn those who in office or in quest of it truckle to an assumed public appetite for easy promises and grand assurances about world affairs.

Machiavelli, for one, saw as an inherent weakness of democratic government the temptation of its leaders to overpromise on their designs in foreign policy so as to marshal support from a public disposed to be indifferent to purposes fitted to reality. This weakness cannot be corrected by leadership alone.

I am reminded here of an account in Bruce Catton's book, *Mr. Lincoln's Army*, of a notable Union brigade's first brush with battle. Mr. Catton recounts: "A regimental historian wrote later that to the end of the war this brigade was always ready for action, 'but we were never again eager.' " How always to be ready to meet the demands of circumstance bearing upon us from the vast external realm without requiring of ourselves the eagerness nurtured by illusion is a big order but one that must be filled if the nation is to do an adequate job of relating itself to the world.

We should adjust our minds to the reciprocalness of alliances and coalitions. I refer here especially to intangibles. Many Americans seem to have more difficulty in accepting the point with respect to them than with respect to the material factors. Often in speaking in public I am asked by someone whether it is true that we are permitting ourselves to be influenced by our allies. The answer is that of course we are. Often the questioner then asks whether by entering into alliances we are not losing freedom. The answer is obvious. We do lose our freedom to act like a nation not belonging to alliances.

One thing we are called upon to recognize is that to generate the consent necessary to maintain coalitions of the free we must interpret our national interest on a basis wider than long experience has accustomed us. It calls upon us to learn, in words of my one-time superior, Mr. Paul Nitze, that "the essence of leadership is the successful resolution of problems and the successful attainment of objectives which impress themselves as being important to those whom one is called upon to lead."

I noted recently in a magazine article by a friend of mine this remark about our world mission: "Americans—of all white peoples—should be best qualified to talk man-to-man with anyone." This leaves out of account something of high moment. Our role entails not simply the need of talking far and wide. That is a relatively easy task. It entails more importantly the duty of listening. The business of listening is much more difficult.

The very assumption of universality implicit in my friend's view somewhat disqualifies us as listeners. In assuming universality we tend also to assume our inherent and obvious rightness. Nothing else so impinges on one's capacity to listen as an assurance of being right beyond peradventure.

Being right, why should we sometimes have so much trouble in getting our friends to agree with us? This question comes naturally to many Americans. In answer, I should say that it is much easier to be right simply on the basis of one's own premises than it is to act rightly when the deed requires the free concurrence of others with diverse points of view. In world politics rightness means not simply to have right ideas in a static way. It means working well and reasonably in an endless process. This is true in domestic politics. It is so in world politics as well.

We Americans tend to make these things too simple.

We admire Davy Crockett's terse formula: "Be sure you're right; then go ahead." That is much too facile for purposes of world politics. The best we can expect is some such paraphrase as this: Be as sure as you reasonably can of the rightness of your premises. Take care as best you can to see that the conclusions which you draw from them are tolerably right. Take adequate account of the legitimate interests and viewpoints of others. After you have done your best to meet these obligations, go ahead as far as the circumstances taken as a whole warrant, getting others to go along as far as you can.

We must adjust our thinking to recognize the greatness of the spans of time required for great creative developments in world politics. In Edmund Burke's words: "Political arrangement, as it is a work for social ends, is to be wrought by social means. There mind must conspire with mind. Time is required to produce that union of minds which can produce all the good we aim at. Our patience will achieve more than our force."

Consent is slow business. We must learn to recognize this. We Americans tend to think of everything as having been accelerated by the processes of modern times. This is not so.

Even in material aspects the retardation of some factors is a function of the acceleration of others. For example, the increase of the speed of airplanes to some eight times or ten times their speed in World War I has multiplied by about fifteen the time required to develop a plane from conception to actualization. Because of the mechanized acceleration of movement and firepower of modern armies it takes some four times as long to train a division as it did only a couple of generations ago. Machines run more rapidly. Brains think no more rapidly. The mind proceeds still at the same old pace allowed by its inherent limits. Thus the concurrence of wills in a process of consent is even slowed by the circumstances of modern times. The range of things necessary for consenting minds to understand and to accept in circumstances of modern world politics is vastly greater. The factors themselves are more complex. The diversity of the minds required to be brought to unison is far wider than in the former periods.

It comes hard to some among us to give up the long love affair—so natural in our youth, so unbecoming in maturity —with the simple solution. According to their persistent counsel, in self-defense we must match the Soviet system in overweening promise and in pretension to having the total answer. This temptation to reach out for all-purpose solutions and to contrive systems of world order purporting to have all the answers for all time must be constantly resisted.

In Justice Holmes' words, "to rest upon a formula is a slumber that, prolonged, means death." It means so in the sense of the fatal inadequacy of all formulas to cope with the ever-changing realities of the power situation in the world. It means it also in the sense that total solutions in politics are inherently totalitarian in their implications and effects. However unexceptionable their motives, the purveyors of total answers in politics are in the last analysis subverters of freedom.

"The great strength of a totalitarian state," Adolf Hitler declared, "is that it forces those who fear it to imitate it." Is it true that totalitarianism can deprive its adversaries of the possibility of choice in such matters? Is it true that our adversary, merely by confronting us with a system of coercion pushed to dogmatic completeness, can foreclose us from the advocacy of consent? Those propositions will be confirmed or refuted only as we choose to act. We must act, however, on the clear assumption of their invalidity. To accept them would be to yield the prize without struggle. Moreover, the guilt of any failure to uphold our values in the world should be clearly recognized as our own and not imputed to the antagonist.

The way of consent looks like the best bet for the long

pull, despite its vexations and uncertainties. It is less rigid, more adaptable, and therefore more durable than a system built upon the primacy of coercion. Let us stand on the premises of the tradition of consent. Let us leave the rest to Providence. Let us keep in mind the wisdom of Herbert Butterfield's words: "The hardest strokes of heaven fall in history upon those who imagine they can control things in a sovereign manner, as though they were kings of the earth, playing Providence not only for themselves but for the far future—reaching out into the future with the wrong kind of far-sightedness . . ."

V

To think and act socially is not a
kind of charity to one's neighbors.
It is a form of self-preservation.
Nor need it become a crusade . . .
Mere intellect is dry and sterile, but
mere devotion reduces everything
to powder, especially if it is bound-
less in scope and starts reform on a
planetary scale. The quest for certainty, the passion for absolutes,
and, even worse, the lustful desire
to enforce the commonest jerry-
built absolutes are . . . a denial
that life is worth living.

—Jacques Barzun,
Of Human Freedom

A Perspective on World Politics

The cab driver on a run from Idlewild to La Guardia Airport on my return from Europe a year ago was one of the more inquisitive members of his calling. He drew forth answers as to whence I had come, where I was going, and what I did for a living. Then came this question: Since I might earn my living in the sensible and uncomplicated business of driving a taxi, why had I chosen a job in the State Department involving continuous subjection to blame for something not my fault—namely the unsatisfactory state of the world?

The cab driver's question was more deferential and edifying than one put to me by a member of a professional audience a while back. This man led up to his question with a long observation. In earlier times, he said, ours was a brave country, standing for something, capable of drawing lines and daring others to step over them, willing to intervene in the affairs of our southern neighbors by interposing the marines, and equal to putting on such daring shows of force as the one of sending the fleet around the world a half-century ago, whereas now—a matter causing deep worry to his friends and him—we seemed to lack the fiber of adventure and the tone of challenge in our external affairs. He asked then what manner of men were my State Department colleagues and I that we had permitted such a decay of will and courage.

The query, designed apparently to give insult rather than to get information, hardly seemed worth answering, for the State Department has been insulted by experts.

Yet I did go into the subject, for I was curious about the real cause of anxiety to him and his friends. It could not really have been a national failure to draw lines for others not to step across. In laying down lines and forbidding aggressive trespass across them, this nation in this decade has been involved in the most extensive development of such character undertaken in any age. It could not really have been a want of having our forces deployed in alien lands. We no longer send marines into neighboring small republics, but the missions of security carried on by our military forces embrace more than half the globe. It could not really have been the absence of circumnavigation of the globe by our fleet. Our naval power now is a main factor in holding open the seas around the globe.

All this I explained to my questioner. I added an observation about the importance of looking at our world problems from a man's standpoint instead of a boy's. He shifted ground right along with me. This, he said, was the very point: The ventures of a few decades ago were briefer, simpler, neater, and less burdensome; and why then should we have given up the delights of our younger days in the world to take on the great and enduring responsibilities of the mature?

The answer, the same in the case of the nation as for an individual, is the one given by a Texas jack rabbit which, under hot pursuit by a hound, climbed a tree, remarking, "This is contrary to my natural predispositions, but necessity leaves no choice." That sets the theme of this closing discourse—the adjustment to present necessity of our national predispositions.

One of the persistent characteristics of the American approach to the problems of world relations in the period of a little more than a half-century since the filling out of the United States' continental position and the development among Americans of an awareness of the United States' attainment of position as a great power has been the notion of the existence of a philosopher's stone in world affairs— an achievable perfect formula capable of solving all the problems and removing all the hazards.

One after another ideas have been brought forth by zealous advocates as panaceas for the world's political infirmities or at least as formulas for redeeming our own portion from danger and uncertainty. Some of the ideas have had elements of validity. These have been exaggerated into excessive significance by the advocates. In other instances the ideas have been inherently worthless and mischievous. Sometimes the government has been involved in the sponsorship. In other instances the formulas for perfect solutions and the movements in support of them have been exclusively of private origin and direction.

The approach of the advocates has invariably been a little careless about the appositeness of the proposed cure to the related problem. Rather than practical and calculating, the mood has usually been emotional and poetic in the sense that poetry involves the suspension of disbelief. Critical judgment in such matters has usually been at a disadvantage. In Edmund Burke's words: "No difficulties occur in what has never been tried. Criticism is almost baffled in discovering the defects of what has not existed; and eager enthusiasm and cheating hope have all the wide field of imagination in which they may expatiate with little or no opposition."

Skeptics airing their doubts have usually been confronted with the question put to the authorities by the proverbial Lisbon peddler taken into custody for selling pills for the prevention of earthquakes: What would you put in their place?

Let us take up a few—only a few, by no means all—of these ideas put forth as perfect formulas for solving the problems of our relationship to the world.

In some phases the grand idea has been to banish the problem of force in world affairs simply by declaring it not to exist.

In roughly the first fifteen years of this century and, with less emphasis, in a period from the middle 1920's to the early 1930's, the idea in fashion was that of establishing world peace through institutions of arbitration and conciliation.

Both are useful devices within limits.

Arbitration has uses in settling disputes of secondary or tertiary importance deemed immaterial to the vital interests of the disputants and therefore not likely to become occasions for armed conflict. It works especially with respect to differences expressible in terms of law and therefore susceptible of being handled in quiet adjudications. Governments generally satisfied with the *status quo* and interested in promoting legal order have often found arbitration useful.

Conciliation is simply a formalized method of mediation. It is useful when exacerbating circumstances have made it awkward or impossible for the disputants alone to settle an issue because of the danger of disadvantage to the party taking the initiative in making concessions. Conciliation merely involves the introduction of other parties into the dispute to attempt to work out an acceptable solution while the disputants mark time.

Zeal gave to these two devices, arbitration and conciliation, proportions and significance far beyond the warrant of reason.

Stimulated by the champions of a systematic solution to the problems of world order, this government persevered on the premise that a structure of world peace, eliminating the institution of war and reducing to a nullity the factors of force in international relations, could be created by establishing permanent international tribunals and weaving a great network of international engagements to resort to arbitration of differences not susceptible of diplomatic solution. Even while persevering in this expectation, however, the government took care—wisely, I am sure—to except from the arbitral obligation all differences bearing on our vital interests, the only sort ever likely to be fought over.

According to our premise in the conciliation movement, it would "hasten universal peace"—Woodrow Wilson's phrase—to have great panels of conciliators standing by and elaborate procedures all worked out by international engagement in advance of any possible quarrels. Our nation industriously built up a treaty system providing such panels and pledging the parties in event of any future quarrels to submit to twelve-month cooling-off periods to permit the panels of conciliators to get in their licks. Even after the outbreak of World War I in 1914 the United States—quixotically, it surely seems in retrospect—still pressed imperial Germany and Austria to engage with us in a mutual promise to cool off for a year before doing anything drastic in event of any future trouble between us and them.

In a period of about thirty-five years, the United States entered into ninety-seven international arbitrational and conciliative contracts. To what practical effect?

The permanent engagements for arbitrations so elaborately worked out with great public éclat have proved

relevant in a few claim adjudications of no moment whatsoever and, if memory serves, in the settlement between
ourselves and other states of two issues of substance. One
case, adjudicated about forty-five years ago, involved the
interpretation of a treaty between the United States and
Great Britain with respect to fishing rights in the North
Atlantic. The other, adjudicated about twenty-five years
ago, related to a dispute with the Netherlands over title
to an unimportant island. Not by even the widest stretch
of the imagination would either issue be considered to
have involved danger of hostilities.

The elaborate machinery of conciliation has proved
useful and relevant in not one single instance.

One may ask whether harm was done by all this effort
so meager of measurable good results. Only the harm—
a considerable one, I believe—of encouraging and pro-
tracting an illusion. This illusion sees great world political
issues as susceptible of being translated into questions
solvable by legal and judicial means. It entertains the
futile belief in strengthening peace by pretending that the
factor of force in the image which nations cast on the consciousness of other nations is not really present.

This notion of solving the problem of force by averting
one's face from it and denying its relevancy, even its
existence, was carried still further in the third decade
of this century in a treaty known to history as the Kellogg-
Briand Pact. An account of the genesis of this treaty would
retell of a prolonged amateur hour in diplomacy—a story
of how a group of individuals, fascinated by tinkering
around with the machinery of states, contrived to press, to
wheedle, and to publicize until they succeeded in pro-
ducing in actuality a multilateral treaty hailed in its day
as giving promise of the consummation of the hope for
perpetual peace. Their idea was extremely simple: to
bring permanent peace at the stroke of a pen, to get all

the sovereign governments merely to plight their word never again to take the initiative in war.

At the instance of many zealots of the quick formula for peace, this devastatingly easy approach was brought forth by the United States government in counter to a French overture of modest character—one for a bilateral treaty between the United States and France expressing in obligative terms the intention of the two nations to abstain from war with each other. Treaties such as suggested by the French government are often made between sovereigns with the intention only to signify amity, not with the expectation of transforming the character of all political relationships. The translation of a proposal for an undertaking of such limited intent into one of general scope and purported significance involved not simply a multiplication of the original idea but a fundamental re-ordering of it. A treaty of pacific intention may express a factual situation as between two or among a small number. As a universal proposition, it states not a fact but a fiction.

The text of the pact still puzzles the discriminating reader. It is ambiguous—an exercise in verbal Indian giving. In one place it purports to foreclose the subscribing governments from war as an instrument of national policy. In another it recognizes the legitimacy of wars fought in self-defense. One wonders whether the pact-makers actually believed in the separability of self-defense and national policy. The answer is that they were apparently under pressure to say something grandly reassuring' and in the circumstances of the time could not take pains to be analytically careful and consistent about how they said it.

In canvassing history for evidence of any positive result of the Kellogg-Briand Pact, we find none. The best we can say of it is to call it barren. Mr. Harold Nicolson, the estimable authority, would say worse of it. He has written of the Kellogg-Briand Pact as having actually been "a danger to international amity" by engendering among peoples "a false sense of security" and by inflating the "diplomatic gold standard of absolute reliance on the plighted word."

In other phases the quest of an all-purpose formula has centered in the idea of transforming international relations through the establishment of a universal organization.

Our brief flirtation with this at the time of the origin of the League of Nations roughly thirty-five years ago is a well-known story. Also well known are the national decision in World War II to reinvigorate the concept of a world organization and, on this second attempt, to go through with our own part in it and the consequences of that decision in the founding of the United Nations. Here, in contrast to the schemes to translate world political problems into legal terms and to solve the problem of force by declaring it nonexistent, the results have been tangible. I shall comment only on some of the exaggerated hopes identified with the effort.

Many of the enthusiastic exponents of the idea of having some central institution as a meeting place where representatives of the world's many governments might congregate regularly to deal with world problems in a concerted way have based their espousal on a suspicion of the usual methods of diplomacy.

Such distrust has generally arisen from two sources. One is the confidential character of normal diplomacy. The second is the tendency of diplomacy to work along lines of particular coinciding interests between two or among a few nations. Many of the champions of universal organization have aspired to substitute open debate for closed negotiations in handling international problems and have also tended to assert some inherent advantage to world order in multiplying the number of nations concerned in any particular issue.

No one at all familiar with the actualities of the United Nations would take at face value the appearances of openness and spontaneity in its deliberations. Quiet diplomacy—accommodations surreptitiously arrived at—is an essential part of its workings. The Wilsonian ideal that "diplomacy shall proceed always frankly and in the public view" is as fictitious in the United Nations as it was in the now departed League. The covert process has not been eliminated. It has only been complicated by the factor of disparity between voting strength in the world's town meeting and power in world realities.

The projection of all differences into open debate, especially within the framework of an organization set up on the basis of a document enunciating moral and legal principles for the governance of world affairs, involves a very real danger of making the positions of disputants inflexible.

This actually increases the obstacles to compromise and temporization. Arthur Balfour's words, spoken almost a half-century ago, on the fallacy and danger of this sort of thing still have wisdom:

"How is the task of peace-maker to be pursued if you are to shout your grievances from the house-tops whenever they occur? The only result is that you embitter public feeling, that the differences between the two states suddenly attain a magnitude they ought never to be allowed to approach, that the newspapers of the two countries agitate themselves, that the parliaments of the two countries have their passions set on fire, and great crises arise, which may end, have sometimes ended, in international catastrophes."

To have to express one's national position in terms of reference of moral and legal standards and in doing so to commit publicly the prestige of one's government sometimes makes it awfully hard to back down even a little bit. Moreover, the idea of having the whole world choose sides on every local issue may often tend only to make large problems out of small ones and to intensify world differences without doing anything whatever to help the parties immediately concerned on toward a solution.

One of the perils of conducting international relations is the temptation to histrionicism on the part of those responsible for conducting them—the temptation to arouse applause, to introduce extraneous emotional elements and elements of exaggeration so as to elicit public enthusiasm. This is perhaps a necessary part of the combative aspects of international relations. Its place in time of war may be justified. It has deleterious effects, however, on procedures intended to lead to accommodation.

This peril of histrionicism is not new to international affairs, but it has become exaggerated in the age of mass communication and the time of mass participation, whether real or sham, in the processes of government. One of the drawbacks of microphone diplomacy—of the conduct of international affairs in large gatherings under full publicity—is the degree in which its usages encourage the theatrical attitude in world relations and tempt vain men and governments to try for grandeur by big talk.

No doubt the use of world forums—with radio, television, klieg lights, and all the other paraphernalia for sending ideas instantly reverberating through the world—is here to stay. The question is how to employ such things so as to avoid worsening the very problems which, in the fond anticipation of its proponents, open diplomacy was supposed to cure.

Fortunately, the need of recognizing the limits of utility in this approach to international problems has drawn increasing notice in recent times. At the opening of the Eighth General Assembly of the United Nations the Secretary General spoke with great wisdom on the need of preserving confidentiality in international affairs and of applying restraint in the use of the international forum.

The American Secretary of State warned against excesses in interposing the United Nations into local issues. The Canadian Foreign Minister spoke shrewdly of the difficulties of glass-house diplomacy, complaining that "open diplomacy now tends to become frozen diplomacy." Similar wisdom came from the French Deputy Minister of Foreign Affairs. Such views mark a retreat from the bright dream of solution by total publicity and by getting every nation possible into the act, but it is a retreat toward reason.

Like every other good thing, the organizational approach to problems of world relations has its limits, and prudence consists in recognizing them. One of the characteristics of great mechanisms is the danger of their coming to dominate the purposes intended to be served. We see this illustrated continuously in modern technology. The life of a family may come to be regulated by the schedules of television. Owners may come to be the servants of their fine new cars. A parallel applies in the field of international organization—the danger of governments' coming to make policy just for the purpose of having something to say from the rostrum. The danger is aggrandized by the notion, now so widely held in important quarters, that foreign policy has no problems that propagandists and public relations experts cannot solve. Mark Twain's distinction between law courts and revival meetings—the difference between manufacturing testimony for the sake of evidence and manufacturing evidence for the sake of testimony—comes to mind. The temptation to do this latter in foreign policy—to make policy for the sake of utterance—is a danger to be guarded against.

In the fourth decade of our century the prevailing fads pertained to the idea of achieving security through withdrawal—of achieving safety by playing it safe; that is, by making ourselves as insignificant as possible as a factor in the power relationships of the world.

One reads now the literature and the debates on international affairs in the 1930's almost with a sense of disbelief. What might happen in regard to factors of power elsewhere in the world was to be of no moment to us. Whether nations friendly or hostile to us controlled the seas and the resources of the continents of the bad old hemisphere was deemed inconsequential. In a favored phrase of the day, America was to be a "pool of sanity"— a sanity presumed to inhere in a complete disregard of the importance of factors of power. America was to sit apart from the world in complete moral self-sufficiency. Others might fight. We would be indifferent to the outcome. The battles over, the victor and the defeated could then lower their buckets and draw up draughts of sanity from our pool to wash away the stains of their transgressions.

One product of the decade in question was a set of neutrality acts.

In Jefferson's time the United States, then a junior, minor, and remote nation, had resorted to embargoes on its commerce with warring Europe for the dual purposes of trying to avoid embroilment and putting pressure on the belligerents to respect our rights. The experiment had failed on both counts. Yet in a time of our greatness this idea was revived and legislated as a standing formula for our conduct whenever the power conflicts of the world might break into open hostilities.

In the words of a sponsoring senator, this was a design for cutting our cables with the Old World in times of danger. With respect to nations in violent contention our significance as a financial source was to be neutralized— that is, nullified. Belligerents were to be denied access to arms, ammunition, and implements of war produced in our country. Commerce with belligerents in other items of supply was to be permitted only when the purchasers

should take title to the goods before they left our shores
and should haul them under other flags. Belligerents were
to be permitted to pre-empt the seas, for we ourselves
would exclude our merchant ships from danger areas.
The arming of our merchantmen for self-protection was
proscribed.

This prescription for ignominy was enacted in several
legislative stages in the period 1935 to 1937. It had over-
whelming and enthusiastic public support and was generally accepted in the Congress as an absolute insurance
of American security in the world. Fortunately, with the
return of the realities of war in the world, the fallacies
of the prescription became apparent. Piece by piece the
misguided formula was thrown overboard from 1939 to
1941. The last significant trace was erased by a generally
unnoted action of the Eightieth Congress restoring explicitly the power of the President to arm American merchantmen for self-protection in time of danger on the seas.

Coincident and generally consonant with the neutrality
acts was a project for amending the Constitution to divest
the Congress of the power to declare war. This had roots
in the extreme expressions of popular sovereignty—initiative, referendum, and recall developed at the level of
the component states of the Federal Union in the early
1900's. During World War I William Jennings Bryan had
espoused a formula for popular control of the war power.
In the period of disillusion after World War I this idea
appeared from time to time in legislative proposals intro-
duced in the Congress. In one embellished version the
formula called for establishing the referendum on war on
a basis of reciprocity with other states; after a stipulated
interval we would cease all relationships, political and
economic, with any nations not concerting with us in the
referendum requirement and any nations not following
suit in breaking relations with the recalcitrants. One
legislator proposed perennially to solve all our problems

by an absolute and unilateral abandonment of the power to make war.

All such proposals found their resting place in the archives. Then suddenly in 1937 a proposal for requiring a referendum on war attracted wide public support and achieved great momentum in the Congress.

It was only a vague idea. The proponents had not even addressed themselves to the mechanics of organizing an electorate for the purpose of counting the votes. They attempted no answer to the question of the consequences of a referendum so close as to make it impossible to determine beyond doubt the prevailing side of the issue. They disregarded the consequences to the nation's international position in event the government should lose on an issue of war after presenting it to the people. They ignored the question of how a government divested of the factor of force in the image cast on minds abroad might command respect for interests under its protection.

Their sole idea appears to have been to insure national safety by divesting our political institutions of essential attributes of government. By not standing on our own feet we would gain an immunity like that achieved by squatting in a game of squat tag. The sponsor of the resolution assured the nation a thousand years in which no foreign country would send its forces across the seas in unprovoked attack. Our power would make us impregnable here. We must detach our concerns from a world in which we could be only a puny factor. Withal, our moral example would have compelling influence abroad. The sponsor portrayed it as "not a fanciful expectation that adoption of the war referendum resolution in America would cause dictatorships to totter" and "tyrants would find themselves bereft of the power to foment wars."

At one stage in the proceedings the war referendum plan enjoyed the suffrage of an absolute majority in the

House of Representatives. The parliamentary vote finally consigning it to the boneyard was carried early in 1938 by a narrow margin of 209 to 188 only after strenuous pressure by the leadership of both major parties—a pressure which, according to reports of the day, shifted fifty-five members of the House from advocacy to opposition at the last minute.

A complete account of our national misadventures and disappointments along paths to Utopia in recent decades would include this government's long persistence in trying to hitch the cart before the horse with respect to disarmament and political accommodation in the 1930's. It would include the story of vain attempts to create a pattern of collective security on the basis of moral abstractions and generalizations. In respect to these concepts, as with respect to other notions of easy ways to ease the course of responsibility, time and experience seem to have had instructive effect.

It would be comforting to be able to report that the time of oversimple diagnosis and overblown cures is all behind us. Circumstances do not warrant such a happy appraisal. There is still occasion for the counsel to regard all schemes for one-shot solutions with that skepticism described by Santayana as "the chastity of the mind—not to be surrendered too easily to the first comer."

We still have among us, though their apparent headway is less now than a few years ago, the exponents of quick total solution by total organization of the world. Their formula usually takes a federal form derived from a misunderstanding of our own federal arrangement.

Our federal mechanism works because the states within its compass have a political likeness to each other and share a universe of discourse. When this failed for a time our federal structure collapsed into civil war. A federal contrivance cannot bridge basic diversity. Those pretending to a solution of the world's political problems by this formula simply base their case on an ignoring of the nature of the problem.

Advocates of this alleged solution are habitually vague on questions of feasibility. Try to get them down to the brass tacks of present reality, and they will invariably go romping off into a wide yonder. Try to talk to them about next steps in policy, and they will answer in leaping generalities. This emptiness of concrete content and this resort to big medicine in preference to specific therapy for particular political ills would be disquieting signs if the impulse in question were formidable enough to be called a movement instead of a hobby.

One more shortcoming should be noted. Legitimate government, let us remember, must rest on a tradition of kingship or aristocracy or on a popular consensus. No tradition of kingship or aristocracy is general to this earth. The elements of an electoral constituency do not exist. Those proposing to solve all the problems by the magic of world government are invariably hazy on the most serious underlying question of government—how to make it legitimate.

We still have with us also exponents of the idea of solving our world problems by transforming our own institutions to get rid of what they regard as the curse of diplomacy. An example of this is a current formula for amending the Constitution so as to establish legislative control of the conduct of foreign policy. This would bring about the supremacy of the particular interests which the Congress represents over the corporate interests of the nation which the Executive must represent in the conduct of foreign policy. More than that, the Bricker Amendment would assign to the legislatures of the component states a concurrent voice whose assent would be necessary before an engagement in foreign policy might have effect in matters reserved to the states under our Constitution, so that with respect to these matters our modes of handling foreign affairs should be restored to what they were under the Articles of Confederation.

As if to exemplify the paradoxicalness of politics, this scheme for a wrenching, disorganizing alteration of our constitutional structure is being purveyed as a formula for strengthening that structure. Revolutionary, disruptive change parades as a plan to preserve things as they are.

What is to become of this mischievous proposition remains for the future, a relatively near future, to settle. Here I wish to speak rather of the past.

I recall a fine little story by James Thurber, the one detailing the secret life of a man named Walter Mitty. His existence is one of perpetual reverie. Life is vital. The world is mundane. Reality is realistic. These qualities Walter Mitty can not suffer. He sets up a world of his own, loftier, more spacious, and less exacting than the real world. All of us have a good deal of Walter Mitty in our characters. This part of us is a refuge. It is also an encumbrance. Daily we have to put aside the Walter Mitty in us in order to engage with responsibility. Each of us has in some degree the problem of not letting Walter Mitty get the best of us. Nations have that problem also.

Alexander Hamilton wrote in *The Federalist* of those "who hope to see realized in America the halcyon scenes of the poetic or fabulous age." He noted the contest in view between them and other Americans of his day "who believe we are likely to experience a common portion of the vicissitudes and calamities which have fallen to the lot of other nations." Hamilton chose sides with the latter. No figure in our historic past exemplifies better than Hamilton such combination of courage and a conservative view of life as enables men and nations to look at the world as it really is and to muster the resources to meet its demands rather than fleeing to a dreamed-up refuge— that attitude spoken of by Keats:

> . . . to bear all naked truths,
> And to envisage circumstance, all calm,
> That is the top of sovereignty.

Hamilton recognized the impossibility of foreseeing or defining "the extent and variety of national exigencies, or the correspondent extent and variety of the means which may be necessary to satisfy them." He observed, "The circumstances that endanger the safety of nations are infinite." He said that "the duties of superintending the national defense and of securing the public peace against foreign or domestic violence involve a provision for casualties and dangers to which no possible limits can be assigned."

In retrospect the nation seems to have been letting what there is in itself of Walter Mitty get the upper hand on the Hamiltonian elements in its character a good deal of the time in the past half-century in problems of relating itself to the vast realm beyond its limits.

For me the most valuable part of preparing these discourses has been to go back over the record of fifty years of the contest between realistic imagination and fantastic imagination in the approach to foreign policy—to trace the rising and vanishing fads and to note the self-assured conclusiveness of their advocates, the unprophetic qualities of what once passed for public wisdom, and history's ironic way of dealing with certitude.

One should sample the opinions and the forecasts of earlier phases not to laugh at the accepted thinkers of days departed but to learn modesty of view in one's own. The elder Oliver Wendell Holmes once described as "the best part of our knowledge" that "which teaches us where knowledge leaves off and ignorance begins." He added, "Nothing more clearly separates a vulgar from a superior mind than the confusion in the first between the little that it truly knows, on the one hand, and what it half knows

and what it thinks it knows on the other." A song familiar
to me as a small boy in Texas put the same thought in
other words:

> You don't know how much you have to know
> In order to know how much you don't know.

The best lesson to be learned from the former prophets
is that there are no experts in world affairs; there are
only those who, by having had to deal responsibly with
affairs of state, have overcome the ignorance of their own
ignorance.

A color of irony emerges in such a review of efforts
toward peace through organizational efficiency and wide
generalization. The nation's diligent and systematic effort
to find a complete solution in arbitration and conciliation
was coincident with that deterioration in international relations leading the world into tragedy of its first encompassing war. Our innocent preoccupation with the
moral strictures of the pact to abolish war and then our
frantic quest for safety in withdrawal via the neutrality
formula coincided with the preparation of circumstances
for the even more destructive World War II. With the
best of intentions, our efforts were wide of the mark.

To some this will suggest that we should have been even
more perseverant toward even grander designs for the
one single idea, all-efficacious and all-encompassing, for
perpetual peace and security. To me it suggests only that
we were working down the wrong line. Our failure was
due to no want of diligence in pursuit of the perfect
formula.

No such formula is possible. The processes of history are
dynamic. They elude the attempt to gain ascendancy over
them by any static design.

This is fundamental to the understanding of foreign
policy. Aristotle's distinction between drama and epic is

relevant here: the one can be brought to conclusion, but the other can only leave off. This is because the one is written whereas the other must be lived. In this sense foreign policy is epic rather than dramatic in character. It is not merely written. It is lived. It cannot be brought to summation and rest. Try as we will, the future will go on tending to get out of hand. In Chesterton's words, "that war is never ended, which defends the sanity of the world against all the stark anarchies and rending negations which rage against it forever." We can best serve by meeting circumstances as they come, trying as well in advance as we can to affect them favorably where we can, reconciling ourselves to the limits but doing our best within them, and keeping in mind the wisdom of Bismarck's description of politics as the art of the next best.

This sense of the contingency of human wisdom and the fallibility of human design in world affairs is not a counsel of despondency and self-defeat. The high hopes of past decades turned out to be unprophetic. The forebodings of the present may turn out to be likewise. The next half-century may have surprises for us just as the past one has had. We have no more reason to be self-assured in a sense of futility than others before us have had in their sense of perfect efficacy.

So I come again to the importance of the principle of self-limitation. I believe it was Goethe who said that to recognize one's own limits is the beginning of freedom. There is more to it than that, however. We must recognize as a nation also the necessity of fulfilling our limits, for as William James said, it is "when we touch our own upper limit and live in our own highest center of energy" that "we may call ourselves saved." Learning these two aspects of the principle of limitation is a lesson which nations, like individuals, must learn in becoming mature.

One of the briefest and clearest accounts of what it means

to grow up is that given by the Apostle Paul in his First Epistle to the Corinthians.

In early years Paul had been identified with a movement dedicated to the idea of realizing a perfect political solution by the establishment of an earthly kingdom fully reflecting the divine will. Then he had come under the influence of other ideas reflecting Hellenistic concepts in their acceptance of the contingent and imperfect nature of historical experience and the inherent ironic character of life. After hard inner struggle, Paul shifted his viewpoint basically in an experience tremendously moving and climactic to the young man himself.

Later, looking back upon the ideas of his younger years, Paul described himself as then having spoken, understood, and reasoned as a child. In his account the great change had come with finding out that in historical experience one could see around and ahead only refractorily at best—"through a glass, darkly" or, as the Greek puts it, "in a riddle." In the words of the epistle, "we know in part," with completeness in knowing and understanding beyond human reach and beyond the scope of history. The learning of this lesson Paul referred to as becoming a man and putting away childish things.

Along with this lesson Paul learned also the meaning of that triad of qualities identified as faith, hope, and charity. The first stands for one's sense of the existence—even though imperfectly perceived—of a meaning of life paramount over and antecedent to one's subjective understanding. The second represents the expectation of some fulfillment transcending one's momentary incapacity to see and to define it in advance. The third represents that compassionate view of other entities and institutions derived from one's knowledge of not having the final answers and one's recognition of all others as being in the same boat.

Paul called the third, the compassionate quality, the greatest of the three.

Let us keep well in mind its paramountcy. It is the quality distinguishing us from our adversary, and we must guard it well. The adversary relies on a system. It contains the elements of faith and hope. Being a system, developed in pretense of having the total answer and in disregard of the inherent limits of all human endeavor and all human wisdom, it forecloses him from compassion.